The Journey of Discipleship

The Journey
of
Discipleship

A Reading of the Gospels

Pierre Simson M Afr.

DOMINICAN PUBLICATIONS

First published (2005) by
Dominican Publications
42 Parnell Square
Dublin 1

ISBN 1-871552-93-1

Cover design by Bill Bolger
from a photo by Philip McShane O.P.

Printed in the Republic of Ireland
by ColourBooks Ltd., Baldoyle, Dublin 13

Contents

Introduction

Among the many images which the New Testament writers use to describe 'discipleship', that is, the life of Jesus' followers, one of the images which speaks to me most is that the life of a disciple is 'a journey.' It is actually the image behind Jesus' call of his first disciples: 'Come, follow me.'

The image of 'the journey of discipleship' appeals to me, first of all because journeying is so much part of our human experience. To me, it means that discipleship, like a journey is in some way an adventure: 'Come, follow me', and I take to the road, not knowing with certainty what tomorrow is going to be, not knowing either where I will be at the end of each day, yet never losing sight of where I am expected to go. And so I have to take each day as it comes, and make the most of it. The ideal is, of course, to keep on walking, 'straining ahead..., racing for the finish', as Paul puts it (Philippians 3:13-14). But actually, a journey is, so often, a succession of thrusts forward and of setbacks. There are times when we decide to sit down rather than walk on; times when we prefer to take short-cuts instead of following the austere main road; and short-cuts, so often too, take us away from the road altogether, and we can waste time and energy walking at random. But all that is part of the venture of a journey, and certainly part of the venture of the journey of discipleship. The patience we are invited to have for ourselves, and for our companions!

For we have companions: a journey, it is true, can be, and is always in some way, a lonely venture; it is 'my' journey. At the same time, however, it is, in very many ways, a community affair; and my companions are my immediate neighbours; the people to whom I can, and should, relate with respect, with discreet and loving concern. Actually, so often, my journey will, at the end of the day, be good or bad depending on how I have tried to relate to my companions, and on how they have responded to me. Now that is so true of the journey of discipleship: 'I give you a new commandment, that you love one another. Just as I have loved you, you also should love one another. By this everyone will know that you are my disciples, if you have love for one another' (John 13:34-35).

But there is more to the journey of discipleship: it is the journey of discipleship because it is a journey we have undertaken on Jesus' invitation, and Jesus, the Risen Lord, is our constant companion. We could say that the journey of discipleship, our journey as disciples of Jesus, is an 'Emmaus experience': the Risen Lord journeys with us, listening to us, sharing our concerns, offering us the light of the Scriptures, giving us, as often as we wish, food for the journey, an Easter journey.

And finally, the journey of discipleship is a journey with a clear direction: it is a journey towards the Father; a journey on which we are constantly accompanied by the Father's immense loving kindness and compassion; the compassion of the father of the parable waiting anxiously for the return of his younger son who has gone away on a journey and has lost his way, and who gives him, when at last he comes back, a breathtaking welcome.

And so, to me, the journey of discipleship is a journey filled with hope: hope rooted in the Father's love, nourished by the presence of the Risen Lord who never tires of telling us, 'in the world, you will have trouble, but be brave, I have conquered the world' (John 16:33).

All I want really with this book is to share with whoever might read it what I have already shared so often and with so many through retreats or Bible sessions: something of my own experience as a disciple who has been journeying on for many years now, but an experience read in the light of the Gospels, in the light of Jesus who is the Way, our way to the Father.

Pierre Simson M. Afr.

The Journey
of
Discipleship

1

'Jesus Stood Among Them'
(*John 20:19*)

'Jesus came and stood among them'

The unifying theme of our reflections in the pages which follow will be the journey of discipleship. The journey on which we embarked when we were 'being formed in our mother's womb', the journey to which our baptism gave direction, the journey on which we plod on with our companions. What we want to do is simply to pause and go back to the source and foundation of our faith, of our call as Christians, religious, missionaries, priests, in order to let the God who called us strengthen us and fill our hearts with renewed love and hope, so that we may journey on and help one another to forge ahead towards the Father's home.

To go back to the foundation and source of our faith is to go back to Jesus—Jesus the Way —and to hear our call from him once again, and to let his love renew us.

We will begin our reflections with two gospel stories which tell us about the two pillars on which our faith, our call, our lives rest: an Easter story, and the story of Jesus' experience at the Jordan before he began his ministry.

'I was dead, and look, I am alive for ever and ever' (Revelation 1:18)

Easter is obviously the very foundation of discipleship. If it were not for Easter, there would be no Christianity, no Church, no mission, no discipleship, no lasting hope. But Jesus of Nazareth is alive, and therefore, the journey of hope can no longer be considered a dream; Jesus, the Risen Lord, tells us, 'Come, follow me', I am the Way to the fulness of life.

But what was Jesus' experience of Easter? Before Jesus' Passover could become his disciples' Passover, it was his own personal experience. How did Jesus, the man from Nazareth, who, in Peter's words, 'had gone everywhere doing good' (Acts 10:38), offering healing and forgiveness to everyone, how did he experience his own passion, death and resurrection?

A Body in a Tomb!

This is how Mark sums up the last hours of Jesus: 'When it was noon, darkness came over the whole land until three in the afternoon. At three o'clock Jesus cried out with a loud voice, "My God, my God, why have you forsaken me?"... Then he gave a loud cry and breathed his last... When evening had come, and since it was the day before the Sabbath, Joseph of Arimathaea went boldly to Pilate and asked for the body of Jesus... Then Joseph bought linen cloth, and taking down the body, wrapped it in the linen cloth and laid it in a tomb that had been hewn out of the rock... He then rolled a stone against the door of the tomb' (Mark 15:33-47).

That is the last image we are given in the gospel of Jesus of Nazareth: a corpse, a body in a tomb; a body broken, wounded, disfigured, a victim to hatred and violence. Humanly speaking, pure waste, the end of all hope!

We must take time to let this image enter into our hearts: the utter failure the tomb of Jesus symbolizes! The waste! It is all over. Once again, hatred and violence, and death have won the day. Whatever miracles Jesus had performed, however beautiful his message, once again, it is all over. As the disciples on the road to Emmaus will put it: 'Our own hope had been... but two whole days have now gone by since it all happened' (Luke 24:21). We have here an experience which is part of our lives: not only the experience of physical death, the deaths of people we love; but also the experiences of failure, of waste, of error, that we all have; our experiences as individuals, as communities, a desert, an exile experience: 'Our own hope had been...'

'I was dead and look, I am alive...' (Revelation 1:18)

But then, the sun rose again for Jesus, the Easter sunrise! And the tremendous cry of joy, of triumph it was for Jesus, when, so to speak, he heard the Father's voice telling him, 'You are my Son, today, I father you again' (Acts 13:33); the cry of joy of the Risen Lord in the Book of Revelation: 'I was dead, and see, I am now alive for ever and ever' (Revelation 1:18).

Jesus, in his human experience, tasting for the first time in the history of humankind, the new life flowing from the Father, thoroughly permeating, transforming his humanness, his whole being, making him wholly new; Jesus feeling in his own flesh the taste of God's victory over hatred, violence, and death. The total victory of God's immense mercy. The Father's loving 'yes' to the whole human experience of Jesus. Nothing that he had lived, that he had done and said, nothing was wasted, nothing was useless; from Bethlehem, and Nazareth to Golgotha, and to the tomb, it had all been life in the making.

Truly, in Dorothy Sayers' words, 'there is no waste with God, God cancels nothing but redeems all.' Perhaps we would say today: God cancels nothing, but recycles all, the total recycling that Easter is.

And because, as Paul puts it, we have been raised to life with Christ' (Colossians 3:1), and his risen life is already ours, our faith affirms that in our own lives too, in the life of our communities, in the life of the Church, there is no waste, ever. God cancels nothing but recycles all.

God's victory at Easter marked the beginning of Christian discipleship: as Christ, through the power of his Father's love, rose to life, the Father could say to the men and women who had followed Jesus during his ministry, and to the multitudes of disciples who were to follow: 'This is my Son, listen to him.'

We will now ask the Evangelist John to tell us about the launching of Christian discipleship and of the Christian mission on Easter day (John 20:19-23).

A Johannine Story

When John wrote his gospel, towards the end of the first century of our era, Christianity had already spread considerably: from Jerusalem to Samaria, to Syria, to Asia Minor, to Rome. There were Christian communities everywhere. Surely, the first

Christian mission had been a remarkable success; a success which was the fruit of much work, much travelling; and many disciples had already paid a very heavy cost, the cost of persecution and martyrdom.

Yet, John could see that the picture of Christianity, at the end of the first century was not all glorious: there were shadows. Yes, it was true, it was obvious, that the early witnesses had worked very hard; and Christian communities were like beehives, full of life and activity. But was it not, too often, at the expense of charity? Work seemed to be the top priority, and little time was perhaps given to relationships, to 'being together.' And as a result, the faith that inspired the apostolic workers was at times a little shallow; the grain had been sown into the ground, but not deeply enough.

John wanted to help the Christians of Asia Minor (present day Turkey) to go back to Jesus, and to learn from him again, as Paul had put it, in his first letter to the Corinthians, that 'of the three things that really matter, faith, hope and love, love is the greatest' (I Cor 13:13). Hence John's insistence, in his gospel, and in his first letter, on relationships: from the encounter near the Jordan between Jesus and the two men who will be his first disciples, to the final encounter between the Risen Lord and Peter on the Lake shore: 'Peter, do you love me?'

John's Easter stories are about relationships first, and mission follows. This is particularly true of John 20:19-23.

The Future Easter Disciples

'When it was evening on that day, the first day of the week, and the doors of the house where the disciples had met were locked for fear of the Jews, Jesus came and stood among them and said, "Peace be with you"' (John 20:19).

John tells us little about the disciples the Risen Lord is about to meet; but what he has to say is important, suggestive.

They were afraid, and therefore, the doors were locked: John will repeat it a little later, 'Eight days later, the disciples were in the house again and Thomas was with them. The doors were closed' (John 20:26).

And the disciples' fear was not inspired by the greatness of the mystery they were about to encounter. They were afraid of the Jews; the fear of tomorrow, after the failure and defeat of yesterday.

Mark and Matthew show the eleven disciples who have assembled around the Risen Lord, doubting to the end.

Thus the disciples who met the Risen Lord were not superhuman, or heroes, or saints, but men and women like us; familiar with 'the tomb-experience' and unable to escape from it by themselves. The Risen Lord did not expect them to be perfect; he did not impose any preconditions on them. He met them just as they were, at the very heart of the reality of their lives, at the very heart of their anguish. That is where he can be found, always. That is a privileged place where he is really present. Jesus, the Risen Lord, with us, 'now, here, now, always.'

'Jesus came and stood among them' (John 20:19)

Jesus the Risen Lord takes the initiative: 'Jesus came and stood among them'; 'you did not choose me, no, I chose you' (John 15:16). And therefore, our trust rests on him, on the initiative of his love.

Jesus the Risen Lord does not come simply occasionally to meet his disciples: now that he is risen, he is always with them, 'yes, to the end of time' (Matthew 28:20). The apparitions of the Risen Lord to his disciples were only the occasional expression of his permanent presence; 'risen', he truly abided in them and they in him. Mark, in his story of Jesus' ministry, loves to call the disciples, 'those with him' (see Mark 3:14). Now that Jesus is risen, 'being with' is the disciples's permanent situation: a disciple is never alone, Jesus is his constant companion, for ever.

And Jesus, the Risen Lord, offers his disciples his great Easter gift: 'Jesus came and stood among them and said, "Peace be with you"' (John 20:19).

The disciples were afraid, Jesus offers them peace. The word 'peace', however, must be properly understood. When war was raging in Bosnia, a few years ago, the town of Sarajevo was very badly damaged. On the evening of the day when a ceasefire was arranged for the first time, in Sarajevo, BBC television showed pictures of a street in the centre of the town: houses, on both sides of the street were in ruins; one could see carcases of cars on the street itself; no one could be seen walking around; the street was totally deserted. The whole picture was one of desolation. But the newscaster commented: 'at long last, there is peace in Sarajevo.' For us, Westerners, this comment made sense in a way: now that a ceasefire had been agreed upon, the conflict had ceased in the town. But the peace Jesus offered to his disciples on Easter day, the peace he offers us constantly, was not, is not, just the absence of conflict. In fact, the disciples of the Risen Lord, as we well know, will meet with opposition, and persecution.

Jesus' peace, the *shalom* of the Hebrew Scriptures, is 'harmony.' It means, feeling at home, at ease with oneself, with God, with one another. It is the peace which is 'harmony in relationships.'

It is so comprehensive that it has to be a gift from God. We simply could not fabricate it; we must receive it: 'Peace I leave with you; my peace I give to you. A peace which the world cannot give, this is my gift to you. Do not let your hearts be troubled, or afraid' (John 14:27).

We must note that the peace offered to the disciples is offered to them by the Risen Crucified Christ: 'Jesus came and stood among them and said, "Peace be with you." After he said this, he showed them his hands and his side. Then the disciples rejoiced when they saw the Lord' (John 20:20).

Jesus' peace is the gift of the Risen Lord to his disciples, but of the Risen Lord still bearing the scars of his Passion; the scars which tell them of the humiliations, the defeat, the failure that the Passion was. Jesus' peace is the gift of someone who knows, and therefore understands. As the Letter to the Hebrews puts it, 'because he himself was tested by what he suffered, he is able to help those who are being tested' (Hebrews 2:18). We have here an image which we must never forget: the Risen Lord does not accuse us, condemn us, because of our failures, and wounds. He knows, he understands. And the certitude of being accepted, understood, is for us a source of deep joy: 'The disciples rejoiced when they saw the Lord.'

It is good and important for us to know that the disciples are going to hear their call to mission in the joy of Easter, in the joy of the Risen Lord who, by the Father's loving grace, has conquered violence, hatred, failure, and even death.

Mission

The ultimate source of 'mission' is the Father: 'As the Father has sent me, so I send you' (John 20:21). This is a typically johannine approach: the relationship which binds the disciples to Jesus is modelled on the relationship which binds Jesus to the Father. And thus, the source of the disciples' mission, of our mission, is, in the last resort, the Father, nothing less. The Father is he whom Jesus came to reveal to the world, the Father who is immense kindness and mercy.

And thus, the mission entrusted by Jesus to his disciples, and to us, is participation in the communion which binds together Father and Son; it is a covenant-oriented mission, a unity-oriented mission, a *shalom*-oriented mission, and therefore, a boundary-breaking mission, a bridge-building mission.

And just as Jesus the missionary was guided by the Spirit — 'The Spirit of the Lord is upon me, because he has anointed me to give good news to the poor' (Luke 4:18) — so are the disciples: 'Jesus breathed on them and said to them: "Receive the Holy Spirit. If you forgive the sins of any, they are forgiven"' (John 20:22).

The Spirit given to the disciples is the Spirit of creation, of the New Creation. We are reminded of the second page of the Book of Genesis, when God, the creator, gave life to the first human being: 'The Lord God formed man from the dust of the ground, and breathed into his nostrils the breath of life; and the man became a living being' (Genesis 2:7).

Through the Spirit given them by the Risen Lord, the disciples are made into 'a New Creation', into Easter disciples, filled with the very life of the Risen Lord; filled with his breath; filled with 'the living water' which becomes a spring within them. In order to become Easter disciples, it is not enough to have met the Risen Lord, to know that the Lord is Risen. One must be born of the Spirit. It is a grace, it is a gift.

And the 'New Creation' is a Creation filled with love, and therefore filled with 'forgiveness': 'Jesus breathed on them and said to them, "Receive the Holy Spirit. If you forgive the sins of any, they are forgiven them; if you retain the sins of any, they are retained."' (John 20:22-23).

Forgiveness was at the very heart of Jesus' mission. The Good News he preached consisted especially in the fact that he invited sinners to God's festive meal. Forgiveness was not for them simply the object of a promise to be fulfilled in the future; through Jesus it was manifested, realized, actualized for them now .[1] What Jesus tells his disciples in the Upper Room is simply: continue my mission.

I like Paul's comment on the New Creation brought about by the Risen Lord: 'If anyone is in Christ, there is a new creation: everything old has passed away; see, everything has become new! All this is from God, who reconciled us to himself through Christ, and has given us the ministry of reconciliation; ...So we are ambassadors for Christ, since God is making his appeal through us; we entreat you on behalf of Christ, be reconciled to God' (II Corinthians 5:17-20).

Thus, the call to discipleship is a call offered to us, given us, by the Risen Lord; our mission is 'filled with the immeasurable greatness of God's power in us who believe, according to the working of his great might which he accomplished in Christ when he raised him from the dead' (Ephesians 1:18-20). There are many instances in our lives when we are tempted to close all doors around us, out of fear. How comforting it is to know that these are moments when the Risen Lord stands nearer than ever, and tells us, while showing us his wounds, 'Peace be with you, as the Father sent me, so am I sending you, in the strength of the Spirit.'

---

1. Joachim Jeremias, *New Testament Theology*, Vol. I, London, SCM 1971, p 113

2

'You are my Son, the Beloved'
(*Mark 1:1-15*)

'When it was evening on the first day of the week, and the doors of the house where the disciples had met were locked for fear of the Jews, Jesus came and stood among them and said, "Peace be with you....As the Father has sent me, so I send you."' (John 20:19,21).

The source of our lives, and of our mission as disciples, is the great Easter Event. But what was Jesus' mission, the mission he wants us to continue? The Evangelists, each one in his own way, invite us to look at Jesus, to listen to him, in order to learn from him what it means to be a disciple, what it means to be sent by Jesus.

We will, therefore, join Peter and Andrew, James and John, on the shore of Lake Tiberias as Jesus of Nazareth was about to meet them and invite them to follow him. But, invited by the four Evangelists, let us first go and meet Jesus himself, near the Jordan river (Mark 1:1-8). Jesus has just left Nazareth, his home town, and we find him lost in the crowd grouped around John the Baptist, listening to the Precursor. Jesus' experience at the Jordan was for him a 'founding experience': it led him to launch later into his own prophetic ministry.

John the Baptist, the Precursor, the Prophet

Who was John the Baptist? John was a prophet; Jesus will say one day, 'much more than a prophet' (Matthew 11:9). That is, someone sent by God on a mission destined for his people. A watchman attentive to God, as all the prophets were, his task was to interpret, in God's light, for the benefit of his people, the meaning of contemporary events.

But John's mission was unique: he sensed that a major 'act of God' was about to take place: the major act of God in human history. God was about to come through his chosen messenger, the Messiah, whose mission it would be to bring about the Kingdom of God, the reign of God: 'As it is written in the prophet Isaiah, "See, I am sending my messenger ahead of you, who will prepare your way; the voice of one crying out in the wilderness: Prepare the way of the Lord, make his paths straight"' (Mark 1:2-3).

John, therefore, called his people to prepare themselves for the great Day of the Lord: they must repent, they must be baptized, and thus form the community which will be ready to welcome Messiah (Mark 1:4-5).

The Messiah, according to John the Baptist

How did John expect the Messiah to be, 'Someone who is more powerful than I am' (Mark 1:7)?

The word 'powerful' here is important: it obviously fits the Messiah and his mission; at the same time, it is a dangerous word, because it can so easily evoke in our minds images which have nothing to do with the gospel. I find it interesting that the word 'power' used by John is accompanied by an image which makes its meaning more concrete: '… and I am not fit to kneel down and undo the strap of his sandals' (Mark 1:7).

And I spontaneously think of a scene described by John in his gospel: 'Jesus, knowing that the Father had given all things into his hands, and that he had come from God and was going to God, got up from the table, took off his outer robe, and tied a towel around himself. Then he poured water into a basin and began to wash the disciples' feet and to wipe them with the towel that was tied around him. He came to Simon Peter, who said to him, "Lord, are you going to wash my feet?" Jesus answered, "You do not know now what I am doing, but later you will understand." Peter said to him, "You will never wash my feet"' (John 13:3-8).

'Power', yes, the supreme power of love, of humble love. John the Baptist sees the Messiah's power manifested in a quite different way: he will usher in the Day of Retribution (Matthew 3:8); the day of God's anger! And therefore, he will be equipped with an axe to fell trees which do not produce good fruit (*ibid* 3:10); with a winnowing-fan to clear his threshing floor (*ibid* 3:12); with fire to burn the chaff (*ibid* 3:12).

We have in all these expressions and images an echo of some of the Old Testament prophets; for instance prophet Amos: 'Trouble for those who are waiting so longingly for the Day of the Lord! What will the Day of the Lord mean for you? It will mean darkness, not light' (Amos 5:18).

And so we have in such texts a typical sample of the way messianic expectations were expressed among good people at the time of Jesus: a 'muscular' Messiah, who would destroy Israel's enemies, would eliminate sinners, and bring God's People to fidelity to the Covenant; a society, a nation which would be truly God's Kingdom. These were John the Baptist's expectations, the expectations of a person who was wholly given to God.

'It was at this time that Jesus came from Nazareth' (Mark 1:9-11)

According to Luke (3:23), Jesus was about 30 when he left Nazareth to go to the Jordan to meet John the Baptist. He had behind him thirty years of silence, spent in a village in Galilee. A carpenter-mason by trade. Little was known about his family: a few names, ordinary, humble people. Little that would make us think of the 'powerful Messiah' expected by John the Baptist.

Jesus' hidden life, as tradition puts it. Jesus , 'in all things like his people, the people of Nazareth, in all things like us, but sin.' And yet, at the same time, Jesus already busy with God's affairs (Luke 2:49). Jesus who, even then, could have said: 'Who has seen me has seen the Father.' And all with the Father's approval, as Easter shows. God's immense simplicity, and humility revealed. So much like us.

But a new page is going to be written in Jesus' life. One day, Jesus left Nazareth to go to the Jordan river and join the people who responded to the Baptist's call: 'In those days Jesus came from Nazareth of Galilee and was baptized by John in the Jordan (Mark 1:9).

Mark does not explain why Jesus left Nazareth to go to the Jordan: but we can presuppose that Jesus has heard about John's movement, and because he was interested and felt concerned, he decided to go and see for himself. And for a time, he was a catechumen of John's, together with other people; listening to John, letting his message, his vision enter into his mind and heart; and thus affirming, living out his solidarity with his people.

And the day came when, again together with other people, Jesus asked for baptism; and thus he entered the community grouped around the Baptist, and intent on preparing for the coming of the Messiah.

We must not pass too lightly over these first steps taken by Jesus of Nazareth onto the public stage on which he is now going to live. These first steps tell us about God's ways, about God's style revealed in and by Jesus. About Jesus' journey among us, about the journey of discipleship.

'You are my Son, the Beloved, My favour rests on you' (Mark 1:10-11)

'And just as he was coming up out of the water, he saw the heavens torn apart': The link is explicitly made by Mark, Matthew and Luke: 'just as he was coming out of the water, he saw...'. Jesus had just joined the messianic community when he was called to enter into another experience which, later, will give his life a totally new direction.

Mark (followed by Luke) sees this experience as a 'personal experience' made by Jesus – 'He saw the heavens torn apart' – and he tries to interpret it for us with the help of symbols which are borrowed from Old Testament stories of encounters between God and his people: 'He saw the heavens torn apart...': Jesus face to face with God, so to speak.

'The Spirit...descending on him...': the Spirit, associated in the Old Testament with creation, 'God's Breath of Life' breathed by God into the first human being (Genesis 2:7); the Spirit of the prophets, 'The Spirit of the Lord is upon me, for the Lord has anointed me, He has sent me to bring good news to the poor' (Isaiah 61:1); the Spirit of God's Servant, 'Here is my servant, I have sent my spirit upon him' (Isaiah 42:1); the Spirit of the Mes-

siah, 'On him will rest the spirit of the Lord' (Isaiah 11:2). Through
the Spirit of God descending on him, Jesus inherits, to bring it to
fulfilment so to speak, the mission of the prophets, of God's Servant, of the Messiah; through him, a 'new creation' will be brought
into being.

'And a voice came from heaven: You are my Son...': the voice
which gives meaning and direction to Jesus' experience: it is
God's voice, the voice of God who steps in; not just God's voice,
but the Father's voice: 'You are my Son, the Beloved, my favour
rests on you.' In a way, these are not new words: in the Old Testament, they, or similar words were addressed to the Messiah, to
the king, to the Just (see Psalm 2; Isaiah 41). They are not meant
either to change Jesus' identity, as if it was now, near the river
Jordan, that Jesus 'became', God's Beloved Son. But they do
confirm him in the relationship which binds him to God, and
this immediately after Jesus has joined the Baptist's movement.

But how did Jesus himself understand these words? What was
his response?

'Abba'! God as Father

As we leaf through the gospels, we may be under the impression
that it was only little by little that the early Christian communities came to understand the importance of the name 'Father'
given by Jesus to God. At least, that is a possible interpretation
of the usage of the name 'Father' for God in the gospels: by the
time John's gospel was written around 100-110, the Johannine
communities saw the word 'Father' as the necessary key to approach the mystery of Jesus' person and mission. As John himself
puts it, 'No one has ever seen God, but the only Son, who is nearest to the Father's heart, he has made God known' (John 1:18).

God as Abba

Jesus' originality, however, was not simply that he called God
'Father', but that he called God 'Abba.' The word 'Abba' expressed, summed up, so to speak, Jesus' response to the voice
heard after his baptism by John the Baptist: 'You are my Son,
the Beloved.'

But what does the word 'Abba' mean? The word 'Abba' is an Aramaic word (Aramaic being the language spoken by Jesus): it was used by small children for their father; its English equivalent would be 'daddy'. It was also used by grown-ups for their father, if their relationship with him allowed it. It could also be used as a title expressing respect: an elder could be addressed as 'Abba'.

I think we can safely say that the word 'Abba' found in the New Testament as a name given to God by Jesus (see Mark 14:36; Gal 4:6; Romans 8.15) should be given the meaning of the word 'Abba' as it was used by small children. And this, especially because of Jesus' insistence in the gospels that 'unless we become like small children, we cannot enter the Kingdom of God' (see Mark 9:35-36; Matthew 18:3; Luke 9:46-48).

Why did Jesus decide to give that name to God?

'Abba' was first the name he gave to Joseph—a word meaning nearness, tenderness, loving support. A word which the Jewish Scriptures never used for God: there did not seem to be any need for it anyway: the Scriptures were so rich, especially when it came to speaking to God or about God; and Jesus, as he grew up was made aware of those riches. Yet, the day came when Jesus decided that 'Abba' was the best name he could give God. And he saw it as summing up beautifully his relationship with God. It also became like the programme of his life, of his mission. As Eamonn Bredin puts it, 'The code word of Jesus, the mystery of his life and person brought to speech: Abba. Familiarity with the Abba-prayer of Jesus makes it virtually impossible for us to recover its revolutionary and shocking impact. Yet Jesus' message and way, his prophetic self-understanding, are compressed into this simple word. Jesus comes across to us as someone who is utterly captivated by God as Abba, as being in love with the Father...' [1]

The code word of Jesus, the code word of Jesus' disciples: 'When you pray, say, 'Abba' (Luke 11:2). Or, as Paul puts it, listen to the Spirit crying out 'Abba' in us: 'Because you are God's

1. 'Discipleship', *The Furrow*, July 1981, p 422.

children, God has sent the Spirit of his Son into our hearts, cry-ing, "Abba!, Father"' (Galatians 4:6).

For a time, Jesus seems to have remained within the Baptist circles. John, in his gospel, even speaks of Jesus and his disciples baptizing, somewhere near the river Jordan, in Judaea, side by side with the Baptist and his own disciples: 'After this, Jesus and his disciples went into the Judaean countryside, and he spent some time there and baptized. John was also baptizing…' (John 3:22).

Which may suggest that it took time for Jesus to fathom, in terms of daily living, the meaning of his experience at the Jor-dan. He had to find out how best to translate 'Abba' into mis-sion and ministry.

It is bound to take time for us to become more and more aware of what it means for us, in terms of daily living, to be Abba's daughters and sons, on a mission from Abba, on their way to Abba's home.

3

'Come, Follow Me...'
(*Mark 1:17*)

Standing there, at my side, as I journey on, is Jesus the Risen Lord. Jesus, Abba's Beloved Son, whose 'code-word' was Abba; whose life-project was Abba. Jesus who had come to tell us the Father's immense kindness and mercy.

And it is this Jesus whom we are now going to meet, on the shore of Lake Tiberias, as he is about to call his first disciples. Thus we are going to go back to the source of our own call. In order to recapture its freshness, its demands and its promises.

The Call of the first Disciples according to Mark – Context

According to Mark's gospel, what could Peter and Andrew, James and John have known about Jesus as he was about to meet and call them? Let us read the first page of Mark's gospel, 1:1-15.

In a way, we could say that this page tells us little about Jesus: fifteen verses suffice to Mark to present John the Baptist and his ministry, and Jesus' experience at the Jordan. Hardly enough to know anyone, to be able to trust anyone.

Yet, according to Mark, these fifteen verses say the essential about Jesus, the essential to which we must constantly go back: 'the good news of Jesus Christ; Jesus, the Father's Beloved Son; Jesus, who has come to usher in the Father's Kingdom...'

And Jesus' first step, as he begins his own ministry is to call the first disciples who will thus be his witnesses from the beginning.

The Story

'As Jesus passed along the Sea of Galilee, he saw Simon and his brother Andrew casting a net into the sea—for they were fishermen. And Jesus said to them, "Follow me and I will make you fish for people." And immediately they left their nets and followed him. As he went a little farther, he saw James son of Zebedee and his brother John, who were in their boat mending the nets. [20] Immediately he called them; and they left their father Zebedee in the boat with the hired men, and followed him (Mark 1:16-20).

Mark's story is extremely short: only 5 verses. And the repetition of the word, 'at once' (1:18,20), a pet word of Mark's, gives the whole scene a flavour of urgency: 'the time has come, the kingdom of God is close at hand' (Mark 1:15); no time must be wasted, 'come, follow me.'

But short as it is, Mark's story does give us again the essentials of the call to discipleship.

Jesus, of course, comes first: there is no discipleship without him, no disciples. He is the subject of most verbs: '*He* was walking along by the Lake, *He* saw, *He* spoke...', the initiative is entirely his, 'You did not choose me, no I chose you' (John 15:16).

His call sounds more like a command than an invitation; there is no dialogue between Jesus and the men he speaks to. It is really Jesus the Lord who calls his disciples. But we must not forget that his authority is that of Abba's loving kindness.

As to the wording of the call, it begins with a command, 'Come': a word which is one of the keywords in any call, beginning with the call of Abraham: 'Now the Lord said to Abram, "Go from your country and your kindred and your father's house to the land that I will show you (Genesis 12:1).

'Come': that is, take to the road, leave the place where you are now; embark on a journey. Not just any journey, however: 'come, follow me.' The journey of discipleship is a journey with Jesus. There must be a 'personal relationship' between the disciples and Jesus; it is not enough to take to the road; a disciple is someone who takes to the road in order to follow Jesus. 'Follow me' gives meaning, direction to 'come'.

Mark does not insist explicitly on this aspect of the disciple's call (neither do Matthew and Luke), but on a number of occasions, in the course of his gospel, he will remind us that the disciples, more especially the Twelve, are 'those with Jesus' (Mark 3:14).

As to the disciples' role in following Jesus, it is expressed in the words, 'I will make you fish for people': this is a strange, enigmatic expression which Mark does not explain. It suggests that, as companions of Jesus, the disciples will learn from Jesus how to become concerned with people. If we want to know in what way people will be part of the disciples' life, we must wait until Jesus effectively begins 'being himself a fisher of people.' For the time being, we simply know that the disciples' life will bind them to Jesus and to people; a twofold relationship to which we will come back later.

How did the men Jesus called on the shore of Lake Tiberias, respond?

Their response was immediate: 'At once, they left their nets...': they have sensed the urgency of Jesus' call, and they make it theirs; the urgency of God's love, 'the love of Christ urges us' (II Cor 5:14); the urgency of the world's needs.

It was this twofold love which gave them the courage to leave behind their possessions, their business, their family; they left everything for a very specific purpose: in order to be able to follow Jesus and to become 'fishers of people.'

This response of the men he had just called was of great importance in Jesus' eyes: he will notice, during his ministry, that the major obstacle to people listening to him, welcoming the Good News, responding to his call, was 'possessions', 'How hard it is for those who have riches to enter the Kingdom of God' (Mark 10:23).

In the course of their journey, the disciples will have to let go again and again of their 'possessions': so many were the things to which they clung, and which hampered, or even rendered impossible, their being with Jesus and their sharing in his mission.

The Story of the Disciples' Call and my Life today

There are four points that I would like to make:

• *We are on our way.*
We have already travelled a great deal, but we know, much better, no doubt, than when we were called, that we still have a long way to go to be 'disciples', totally. We are on our way, we must journey on; though we are, at times, tempted to sit down and

give up. And Jesus' call reaches out to us, 'come.'

It is good to know, essential even, that the Jesus who calls us is not a slave-driver, but Abba's Beloved Son, and that his insistence, 'come', is that of his love.

• *Fishers of people': Jesus' experience*
To become a disciple means to enter into a twofold relationship: relationship with Jesus ('follow me') and relationship with people ('I will make you fish for people'). This latter expression is made quite clear in Mark's account of the beginning of Jesus' ministry: Let us read this account (Mark 1:21-39).

We could say that this story aims at answering the question which the very first Christians must have often put to the disciples who had known and followed Jesus: what did Jesus do? How did he spend his time? - Mark answers them: 'let me tell you about a day in the ministry of Jesus.' And the day described by Mark is a Sabbath day.

If we take Mark's story just how it stands, this is how Jesus' day unfolds: On Friday evening, Jesus who has just arrived in Capernaum with Peter, Andrew, James and John, goes to the Synagogue for the opening of the Sabbath (Mark 1:21-28). There, *he teaches*. Mark does not give us the content of Jesus' teaching, but simply points out that Jesus taught with authority; teaching was very much part of Jesus' mission, of Jesus' approach to 'fishing for people.'

Jesus also *heals* a man possessed by a demon: thus, at the very beginning of his ministry, Jesus faces evil, the forces of evil at work in the world in so many different ways, and Jesus feels concerned, and heals, not just expelling the demon, but healing the possessed man, and giving him to enter once again into the mainstream of social life.

Again on Friday evening, but after the synagogue service, Jesus goes to Peter's house to share the Sabbath meal with his disciples and Peter's family (Mark 1:29-31). Obviously, Jesus and his disciples expect to find the meal ready; but Peter's mother-in-law, who was supposed to have prepared the meal, is in bed, sick with a fever. Again Jesus feels concerned about her, and therefore, as Mark puts it beautifully, 'he came and took her by the hand and lifted her up', he healed her. The rest of the Sabbath day, i.e. our Saturday, Jesus, who is a practising Jew, rests.

But on Saturday evening, after sunset, as the Sabbath is over, many sick people are brought to Jesus, and he heals them (Mark 1:32-34).

Finally, on Sunday morning, 'in the morning, long before dawn', Jesus goes to a lonely place and prays (Mark 1:35).

Let us reflect a moment on this 'day in Jesus' ministry'; the ministry of the Jesus we have been called to follow.

Jesus and the sick.[1] In Jesus' time, among the Jews, the sick, the mad, the disfigured were often seen as being punished by God for their sin. We remember the question put to Jesus by his disciples when they saw the man born blind in Jerusalem: 'Rabbi, who sinned, this man or his parents, that he was born blind?' (John 9:2). Sick people, therefore, not only had to bear the physical pain caused by their illness; they were also made to feel guilty.

If their disease was contagious, they were banished from normal family life, from their job, and their usual social settings. All human contact had to be avoided. The desperately ill of these times were fiercely isolated. They were true outcasts in this society.

Jesus was obviously aware of that situation: how many times had he already seen and met sick people during the 30 years he had spent in Nazareth. But now, *for the first time,* he was committing himself publicly to work at making God's Kingdom visible, at making 'Abba' become reality in the lives of people; in Abba's kingdom, there cannot be any outcasts. Jesus could not therefore avoid doing something practical about this distressing reality

It is against that background that we must look again at the extraordinary scene described by Mark: 'they brought to him all who were sick and those who were possessed by devils. The whole town came crowding round the door ' (Mark 1:22).

It had not taken long for people, for the sick, to sense that something new was happening; they seemed suddenly to realise that no one but Jesus could possibly heal this weeping social sore. This was their one chance, their one and only hope. Here was someone who treated the disfigured, the sick and the mad with a sacredness and dignity that they experienced nowhere

1. See Frank Andersen MSC, *Jesus, our Story,* Dove 1994, p 19-22.

else. He gave them hope.

For Jesus, it was a new, wonderful experience, facing all these sick people, reading both despair and hope in their eyes. Luke writes, in his own story, 'he laid his hands on each of them and cured them.' (Luke 4:40). It was through Jesus' healing touch and healing words that Abba's Kingdom became real for all those people.

•. *Jesus' Prayer*

As Mark presents it, Jesus' prayer seems to be connected with his experience of the Sabbath, and especially the experience of the evening of the Sabbath day: 'In the morning, long before dawn, he got up and left the house and went off to a lonely place and prayed there' (Mark 1:32).

He had just experienced two things: first, the horror and desperation of so many broken people, he had glimpsed for the first time in his life the full extent of human need and suffering. And Capernaum was only one town among many. He had also experienced power in himself, the power of his compassion: his touch had healed the sick.

These two experiences drove Jesus to prayer: he had to meet Abba face to face to let Abba's merciful love throw light on the new step he had taken. And in Abba's light, he saw that he had been given only the merest glimpse of his people's massive neediness. What he had seen in Capernaum was going on in every village and town. To be true to Abba's heart and to his own, he must get going. It was urgent: 'Let us go elsewhere' (Mark 1:38).

• *'I will make you fish for people'*

Let us now read our experience as 'disciples' in the light of this page in Mark's Gospel. It obviously concerns us as disciples of Jesus.

We are called to be 'fishers of people': that is, we are bonded to God, to Abba through Jesus; but also, like Jesus, bonded to people; called to be, like Jesus, 'people for others.' People must have a prominent place in my life, especially those who are most in need of help, of comfort, of healing.

We are, therefore, called to teach, like Jesus, but in the way that corresponds to our 'vocation', our 'situation'. We might not be 'professional religion teachers', but as disciples, we are called to share our faith with one another, with the people we meet, who are part of our lives. In Jesus' words, we must be 'salt for the earth, light for the world' (Matthew 5:13-16).

And that is a challenge for us: in order to share our faith with people, we must endeavour to live what we want to share, we must know what we want to share. And we must share our faith in such a way that people understand us, feel concerned by and interested in, what we share with them. It belongs to us to make the gospel 'desirable.'

Like Jesus also, we are bound to be confronted with evil in the world: for there is evil around us, in us; the Gospel invites us to be realistic about it, not naive. Not just realistic, however, but also optimistic, the optimism of faith: 'In the world, you will have trouble, but be brave, I have conquered the world' (John 16:33). As to how we are to confront evil, Jesus shows us the way: Jesus was not content, as we often are, to lament about the active presence of evil in the world; he did denounce it, but he also fought against it, especially perhaps, through his healing ministry. He died that we might have life and have it to the full. The gospels cannot answer all our questions concerning our battle with evil today, but they certainly tell us about the spirit which should inspire us, the Spirit of Jesus.

And thus, as Jesus' disciples, we are called to bring healing to the sick, to the poor, to the marginaised, beginning with those in our immediate community. They must have priority because, more than anybody else, they need to be helped; more than anybody else, they need to experience Abba's loving kindness.

But can we really offer healing to people? There are people, in our Christian communities, who like Father Tardif, or Sister Breege McKenna, are gifted with a special gift of healing. But we are all, without any exception, basically equipped with a healing gift; actually the gift of healing without which all forms of healing would be found wanting; the gift of love which 'has been poured into our hearts by the Holy Spirit who has been given to us' (Romans 5:5). In that sense, we are all 'healers.' 'Wounded healers' who also need healing.

It is this love in me, Abba's love, which allows me to approach people, especially the sick, the poor, the marginalised, not to condemn them, to despise them, but to share with them Abba's immense healing kindness and mercy.

'Come, follow me, and I will make you fish for people': I must listen attentively, at length, to these words; they must become more and more my programme, as they were the programme of the first disciples Jesus called on the shore of Lake Tiberias.

And I must never forget that the always necessary 'testing ground' will be my immediate community.

4

'Come and see...Abide with me'
(*John 1:19-42*)

From Mark to John's Gospel

As we were reflecting on Mark's story of the call of Jesus' first disciples, we noted that that call sounded somehow like a command, the command of a Master to his servants: 'Come, follow me, I will make you fishers of people.' And we also noted that Mark seemed to put the stress, in the first page of his gospel, not so much on the relationship which binds a disciple to Jesus, as on the disciples being taught how to be 'fishers of people.'

John's approach is different: as always in his Gospel, he puts the stress on the personal relationship which must bind a disciple to Jesus and the disciples to one another. Why this stress on relationships? Perhaps was it due to John's personal experience: he was someone for whom 'relationships' were the essential. Perhaps also was it a consequence of the assessment he could make of the life of the Christian communities at the end of the first century: there were Christian communities everywhere—in Judaea, and Samaria, and Galilee, and Syria, in Asia Minor, in Greece, in Rome; the Good News had spread so rapidly. Yet, how deep had the Lord's command gone into the minds and hearts and lives of Christians: 'Love one another... It is by the love you have for one another that everyone will recognise you as my disciples' (John 13:34-35)? Judging from John's first letter, there were divisions among Jesus' disciples. Not only had the first heresies already appeared in a number of communities, but even among faithful Christians, fraternal love was so often found wanting (see I John 3:11-18).

Whatever the cause, John certainly went out of his way to stress again and again the importance of relationships. And we find evidence of this in John' story of the call of Jesus' first disciples.

The Context of the Call of the Disciples in John's Gospel

The four Evangelists place the call of Jesus' first disciples at the beginning of Jesus' ministry, but each one of them leads up to his story in his own way (compare, for instance, Matthew 4:12-22 and Luke 5:1-11). How does John introduce his own story?

'In the beginning was the Word, and the Word was with God, and the Word was God. (John 1:1). John invites us to go back to the 'ultimate source' of all that exists: the very mystery of God.

And more precisely, the mystery of a God who 'speaks', who communicates, a God who 'makes' communion; the God of whom John will say, in his first letter, that 'God IS love' (I John 4:8).

We know the importance of 'God's Word' in the Scriptures: the God of the Scriptures is a God who speaks, who speaks unceasingly, and who expects a response. Perhaps could we try to approach this mystery in the light of our own experience of communication in our own lives: we know how important communication is between people, between the members of a family, of a community. We need to communicate with others, to speak to them, to feel that we are being listened to; and if we cannot communicate, we feel so unhappy. On the other hand, communication is not all that easy: at times, we fail to communicate because people do not understand us; or then, they may misunderstand us, and we feel frustrated. Communicating is a risky business, so risky that at times, we prefer to keep to ourselves; but that too soon becomes intolerable. We must therefore say that 'communicating', 'speaking', is vital, but it can be, and often is, dramatic; it can give us great joy, when we feel understood, when people respond positively to us, when we feel we are in loving communion with one another. But speaking, communicating can also be for us the cause of many wounds.

What can that experience tell us about God, the God of John's Prologue? Reading the first page of John's gospel, we are given the impression that God wants to speak, wants to communicate at all costs, so to speak. The creation of the universe is like God's first attempt at 'communicating': 'In the beginning was the Word, and the Word was with God, and the Word was God. He was in the beginning with God. All things came into being through him, and without him not one thing came into being. (John 1:1-3).

The universe mirrors God's greatness. It is an expression of God's mystery, a vision which the Psalmists sing beautifully: 'The heavens are telling the glory of God; and the firmament proclaims his handiwork. Day to day pours forth speech, and night to night declares knowledge (Psalm 19:1-2).

But God did not simply want to speak; God wanted a response: God, therefore, chose a people, Israel, which would be God's privileged partner in an unceasing and dramatic dialogue: 'The true light, which enlightens everyone, was coming into the world. He was in the world, and the world came into being through him; yet the world did not know him. He came to what was his own, and his own people did not accept him' (John 1:9-11).

God, however, did not take 'no' for an answer: 'when the completion of the time came' (Galatians 4:4), God took a final step: 'And the Word became flesh and lived among us, and we have seen his glory, the glory as of a father's only son, full of grace and truth' (John 1:14).

God become one of us in Jesus, speaking our own language, within our own experience, and therefore enabling us to understand him and to respond to him.

Not just the 'Word of God', however, but the 'Word of the *Father*': 'No one has ever seen God. It is God the only Son, who is close to the Father's heart, who has made him known' (John 1:18). Thus, in Jesus, it is God, Abba, who speaks and asks for a response.

In the light of John's reflection on the mystery of God's Word, we can understand the call of Jesus' first disciples—and therefore our call—as an invitation to enter actively into the mystery of God seeking, out of love, to communicate, to enter into communion, with humankind. To enter actively into the mystery of God-made one of us, the mystery of Jesus, the Word of God made flesh.

'A voice of one that cries in the desert'

In Mark (1:16-20) and in Matthew (4:18-22), it is Jesus himself who goes to the future disciples and calls them: the initiative is totally his: he calls, they answer! We could say that Mark's and Matthew's stories simply give us the basic pattern of a call, of any call, rather than the very human experience of the four men Jesus met on the Lake Shore and called to follow him. Usually, things do not happen that way in our world.

Luke (5:1-11) does make the experience of the disciples' call more human: Jesus wants to speak to the crowds, he asks fishermen to lend him a boat from which he will speak; once his teaching is over, Jesus invites the fishermen to throw their nets into the Lake, and they are rewarded with a miraculous draught of fish; then, and only then, does their call take place.

Let us now read John's story I:35-45. We must certainly say that John, in his Gospel, constantly stresses that Jesus is truly, as the Nicean Creed will proclaim, 'God from God, light from light, true God from true God'. But again and again, John also insists on how human Jesus is: the Word of God, yes, but *made flesh*. This is obvious in John's story of the call of Jesus' first disciples.

Their call is not just an affair between Jesus and each one of them; it takes place within the context of a whole network of relationships: Jesus meets Andrew and another disciple through John the Baptist; it is Andrew who brings Simon to Jesus; and if Philip is called directly by Jesus, Philip becomes an intermediary between Nathanael and Jesus. It is so much like our own human experience: God's word, and call reach us through events, especially through people; we all can be 'mediators of encounters' with people, with Jesus, with God; provided, of course, we do not screen off Jesus. John seems to see John the Baptist as an ideal go-between (John 1:19-34):

'I am not the Christ.' John the Baptist's insistence is worth noting. He has an important role to play as the precursor whose mission it is to present the Messiah to the world, but it is a role which is wholly dependent on, related to, the person of the Messiah. He will not screen off the Messiah, take his place; all he wants is to point out the Messiah!

Therefore, he is attentive, sensitive to the Messiah's presence: in his gospel, Luke saw this sensitivity as characteristic of John even in its mother's womb: 'As soon as I heard the sound of your greeting, the child in my womb leaped for joy' (Luke 1:44).

We find the same attitude in the adult John the Baptist: 'John answered them (the people who had been sent to ask him who he was): "I baptize with water. Among you stands one whom you do not know,... Here is the Lamb of God who takes away the sin of the world"' (John 1:26, 29, 36).

It is he, and he alone who matters. John does not keep anything to himself, and as he points to the Messiah, his own disciples leave him to follow Jesus: 'The next day John again was standing with two of his disciples, and as he watched Jesus walk by, he exclaimed, "Look, here is the Lamb of God!" The two disciples heard him say this, and they followed Jesus' (John 1:35-37).

John's role was most difficult, demanding great abnegation. The Evangelist seems to suggest what John's spirituality was what inspired him: 'You yourselves are my witnesses that I said, "I am not the Messiah, but I have been sent ahead of him." He who has the bride is the bridegroom. The friend of the bridegroom, who stands and hears him, rejoices greatly at the bridegroom's voice. For this reason my joy has been fulfilled. He must increase, but I must decrease' (John 1:35-37).

It was love, the love of Jesus that made John the Baptist such a good precursor, a good go-between. His spirituality was a covenant-spirituality. He was the bridegroom's friend. We have here a programme for Jesus' witnesses, Jesus' disciples.

The Encounter between Jesus' and John's disciples

'The next day John again was standing with two of his disciples, and as he watched Jesus walk by, he exclaimed, "Look, here is the Lamb of God!" The two disciples heard him say this, and they followed Jesus... (John 1:35-39).

It was an encounter, not just a 'call': at John the Baptist's words, two of his disciples took the initiative of 'following Jesus'; Jesus, somewhat surprised, turned and asked them: 'What do you want?' A question which we may understand as an invitation given to the two men to be aware of the meaning and purpose of their decision 'to follow' Jesus.

Their answer expresses their desire to meet Jesus, to take time to know who he is: 'Where are you staying?' And Jesus simply says to them: 'Come and see.' There is not a word about being taught how to become 'fishers of people.' Rather, an encounter will take place, a personal encounter which will allow the people involved to learn about each other. It will be the beginning of an I-Thou relationship which will blossom into friendship (John 15:14-15).

Where are you Staying?

It takes time for people to come to know one another: and John underlines that through the use of the verb 'to stay' which I would like to change into 'to abide' because I feel that the word 'to abide' has richer undertones than the very prosaic word 'to stay': 'When Jesus turned and saw them following, he said to them, "What are you looking for?" They said to him, "Rabbi where are you staying" [Where do you abide?]. He said to them, "Come and see." They came and saw where he was staying [where he abode], and they remained [they abode] with him that day. It was about four o'clock in the afternoon.' (John 1:38-39).

The verb 'to abide' appears three times in two verses: it is a favourite verb in John's gospel in which it occurs thirty seven times (against twice in Mark, three times in Matthew, and six times in Luke).

What is its meaning in John's gospel? It expresses, so often, 'relationship', 'personal relationship'; that is certainly the case in John ch. 6 and ch. 15. And I see two major characteristics in the relationship thus indicated by the verb, 'to abide': first, it suggests 'intimacy', 'at-oneness', 'life-giving communion': 'Abide in me as I abide in you. Just as the branch cannot bear fruit by itself unless it abides in the vine, neither can you unless you abide in me... As the Father has loved me, so I have loved you; abide in my love. If you keep my commandments, you will abide in my love, just as I have kept my Father's commandments and abide in his love' (John 15:4, 9-10).

It also suggests 'time', 'duration'– the time needed for life to unfold, for friendship to grow; for fidelity to have roots. The time we are perhaps so reluctant to take, to give, nowadays: we are so much in a hurry, whether it be in our relationship with God, or in our relationship with one another in our communities. We are used to 'instant coffee', to planes flying at the speed of sound, to MacDonald's 'instant hamburgers' Perhaps we also try to have 'instant relationships', 'quick encounters' which, however, will finally leave us alone.

It took three years for the disciples whom Jesus had met near the Jordan, to be sent on their first mission (John 20:21). For them, the time of Jesus' ministry was 'time for abiding with Jesus.'

'Infinitely more than we could ask or imagine...' (Ephesians 3:20)

What did they learn from Jesus? There is in us a tremendous longing for life, for more life, for better life; we never say, 'enough.' But God, who has created us in his own image and likeness, is the God of Life, 'lover of life', as the Book of Wisdom puts it (Wisdom 11:26), and God has sent Jesus into the world 'that we may have life and have it to the full' (John 10:10).

In John's gospel, in all his encounters with people, Jesus seeks to meet people's needs, desires and longings, but always in order to open their hearts, their lives *wider* to the immense riches the Father has in store for them. At Cana (John 2:1-12), all that the guests at the wedding feast wanted was enough wine to celebrate; Jesus gave them thirty gallons of the best wine, but it was only a foretaste of the gift he was to make later: 'Then he took a cup, and after giving thanks he gave it to them, saying, "Drink from it, all of you; for this is my blood of the covenant, which is poured out for many for the forgiveness of sins"' (Matthew 26:27-28)

Or, in John's words, 'Those who eat my flesh and drink my blood have eternal life, and I will raise them up on the last day; for my flesh is true food and my blood is true drink. Those who eat my flesh and drink my blood abide in me, and I in them' (John 6:54-56).

Nicodemus (John 3:1-8) came to see Jesus at night wanting to know more about Jesus; Jesus offered him new life, a new birth.

To the Samaritan woman the water in the well of Samaria was of vital importance. Jesus who had asked her to give him a drink understood her; but he wanted to offer her much more: 'living water welling up in her into eternal life' (John 4:14).

Jesus offered always more than people dared to desire, to ask for or imagine! It was the disciples' daily experience. They had joined the movement launched by the Baptist because they longed for the Liberator who was about to come. John directed them to Jesus. They followed Jesus; they wanted to meet him: 'Where do you abide?... Come and see.' And they found that the man from Nazareth— 'from Nazareth? Can anything good come from that place? (John 1:46)—was indeed the Messiah: 'We have found the Messiah' (John 1:41,44).

It was for them the beginning of a journey which led them to discover in, and through Jesus, the endless wonders of God's love. Jesus' words to Nathanael express so well what their experience was, what our experience can be: 'You will see much more'; infinitely more, because you have been created for much more, for infinitely more: by God, and for God.[1]

'We have found the Messiah'

'The two disciples heard him say this, and they followed Jesus... They came and saw where he was staying, and they remained with him that day' (John 1:35-37).

We would love to know what Jesus and the two men did that afternoon, what they talked about. But we do know what the fruit of the encounter was for the two disciples: 'One of the two who heard John speak and followed him was Andrew, Simon Peter's brother. He first found his brother Simon and said to him, "We have found the Messiah"' (John 1:40-42).

Later, Philip, who had been called by Jesus (John 1:43), 'found Nathanael and said to him, We have found him about whom Moses in the law and also the prophets wrote, Jesus son of Joseph from Nazareth' (John 1:45).

Having met Jesus, having 'abided' with him, the disciples could not stop proclaiming what they had seen and heard' (see Acts 4:20).

'Come, follow me, I will make you fish for people' (Mark 1:17). 'Come and see, abide with me, and the day will come when I will send you out as the Father has sent me' (see John 1:39 and 20:21).

1. For all this, see Eloi Leclerc, *Le Maître du Désir*, DDB 1997, p 23-30.

Both gospel stories, Mark's and John's, are our story. We must take time to read them in the present tense in order to allow them to challenge us. Like Nathanael, we still have so much to learn: 'You are going to see greater things than that' (John 1:50).

5

'If you only knew what God is giving'
(John 4:1-26)

In their story of the call of the first disciples, Matthew, Mark and Luke show us Jesus telling the four men he has met on the Lake Shore: 'Come, follow me, and I will make you fish for people.' John, as we have seen, prefers to present Jesus' mission as a mission of 'revelation': 'No one has ever seen God, but the only Son who is nearest to the Father's heart, has made him known' (John 1:18).

The Johannine Jesus, therefore, invites his disciples to 'come and see', 'to abide with him'; and he will lead them to discover progressively the immense treasures of the Father's love: 'You are going to see greater things than that' (John 1:50). You are made for much more, you are made for God. Let the Father open your minds and hearts to the measure of his love. And the day will come when you, in your turn, will be sent to continue my mission: 'As the Father has sent me, so am I sending you' (John 20:21).

Early in the fourth gospel, we find three stories which illustrate particularly well this message of the Johannine Jesus. John writes about three encounters: Jesus meets a Jew, Nicodemus (3:1-21); he then meets a woman from Samaria (4:1-42); and finally, he meets a pagan who was a royal official in Capernaum (4:46-54). We will focus our attention on the second encounter.

A Difficult Encounter

'Jesus left Judea and started back to Galilee. But he had to go through Samaria. So he came to a Samaritan city called Sychar... Jacob's well was there, and Jesus, tired out by his journey, was sitting by the well. It was about noon. A Samaritan woman came to draw water, and Jesus said to her, "Give me a drink." The

Samaritan woman said to him, "How is it that you, a Jew, ask a drink of me, a woman of Samaria?" (Jews do not share things in common with Samaritans)' (John 4:3-9).

We could say that as Jesus begs the Samaritan woman for a drink, he comes up against two major difficulties: it was not normal for a man to meet a woman alone in a public place and to speak to her. Later, when the disciples returned from the nearby village, 'they were surprised to find Jesus speaking to a woman' (Jean 4:27). The second difficulty is the woman at the well was a Samaritan; she belonged to a people whom the Jews despised because, due to historical circumstances, Samaria no longer belonged to the Covenant Community of God's People. The Samaritans were a mixed race and considered as heretics by the Jews. We have an echo of that situation, and of the way the Jews looked down on Samaritans in this short passage from the Book of Ben Sirah: 'There are two nations that my soul detests, the third is not a nation at all: the inhabitants of Edom (South of the Dead Sea), and the Philistines (on the coast), and the stupid people living in Shechem (Samaria)' (Ben Sirah 50:　　25-26).

It will take time for the woman to accept Jesus, the man, the Jew.

The conversation between Jesus and the Samaritan woman unfolds around two important symbols: Jacob's well and the place where one ought to worship God. Let us allow these symbols to guide our reflections.

From the Water of Jacob's Well to the 'Living Water' of the Spirit

John continues in verse 10: ' Jesus answered her, "If you knew the gift of God, and who it is that is saying to you, 'Give me a drink,' you would have asked him, and he would have given you living water." The woman said to him, "Sir, you have no bucket, and the well is deep. Where do you get that living water? Are you greater than our ancestor Jacob, who gave us the well, and with his sons and his flocks drank from it?" Jesus said to her, "Everyone who drinks of this water will be thirsty again, but those who drink of the water that I will give them will never be thirsty. The water that I will give will become in them a spring of water gushing up to eternal life." The woman said to him, "Sir, give me this water, so that I may never be thirsty or have to keep coming here to draw water"' (John 4:10-15).

Jacob's Well

Listening to the woman, we realize how important the well of Jacob was to her. In a dry country, a good well which has been giving water faithfully for centuries means security for daily life; it symbolizes what is essential for life. From that point of view, the woman does not need anything from this man who has just spoken to her.

But Jacob's well is not just for the woman a source of water: it also symbolizes the community to which she belongs, her people; the well is like the centre of the community, it makes community living possible; the village to which she belongs is made possible by the well; and the well is a meeting point for people, especially for women who, day after day, go down to the well to draw water, and to have a chat with one another. The woman is not alone; she has a community, whose ancestors are famous, ancestors whom the Jews themselves know and revere.

In a way, this woman is satisfied. As long as Jacob's well gives her water, she feels secure.

'Give me a drink'

How will Jesus overcome the barriers, which seem to make it impossible for him to fulfil his mission, 'to reveal the Father to this woman'? How is he going to help the Samaritan woman to go beyond, to open her heart to the wonderful riches he has in store for her?

'Jacob's well is there and Jesus, tired by the journey, sat straight down by the well; it was about the sixth hour (noon)' (John 4:6).

A few words suffice for John to show us the simple reality of the 'incarnation' of God's Son in daily life. Jesus tired by the journey, at midday in the hot plain of Samaria, is sitting near the well, with water, cool water a few feet from where he sits; and he is terribly thirsty.

Every word matters: tired, sitting (not standing, which would have give him an advantage over the woman), thirsty; and there is nothing he can do about it. If only he could have some of the water from the well to quench his thirst: 'From rich he became poor to make us rich out of his poverty' (II Corinthians 8:9).

And thus Jesus is cornered into begging the woman for water: 'Give me a drink': quench my thirst, please! And that simple request opens the way for the confrontation between the woman and Jesus to become an encounter. Now Jesus is no longer for the woman a man who pushes women around; he is no longer an arrogant Jew who despises Samaritans; he is no longer a religious Jew who considers Samaritans as unclean, and avoids contacts with them. Rather, he is, before her, a fellow human being in need of help, asking for help. Jesus' request to the woman was a call to the woman's humanness beyond the barriers of sex, race or religion.

That is the reality of the incarnation: Jesus, near Jacob's well, Jesus at Gethsemane, Jesus at Calvary (crying out 'I am thirsty!' John 19:28); Jesus in solidarity with the poor, and marginalised, and sufferers of our world; one of them, sharing their needs, their longings, their desires, their thirst, their hunger. God revealed, the Father revealed.

'The water that I shall give...'

Now that the woman's reluctance to respond to Jesus' request has been overcome, Jesus can invite her to go further on her journey.

Jesus obviously knows, especially now as he drinks from the water given him by the woman, the price and value of the water in the well; and whatever the gifts he has come to offer us, they do not cancel the 'gift of water.'

But as always in John's gospel, 'revelation' begins from 'human experience', from the human reality which is already pregnant with God: 'There is the dearest freshness deep down things' (Gerard Manley Hopkins).

It is this 'dearest freshness' that Jesus now wants to reveal to the woman: 'If you only knew what God is offering, you would have been the one to ask and he would have given you living water... Whoever drinks this water will get thirsty again, but anyone who drinks the water that I shall give will never be thirsty again; the water that I shall give will turn into a spring inside him, welling up to eternal life' (4:10,13-14).

We note first the recurring verb 'to give': a verb which plays a major role in John's gospel; while we constantly try to forge our own lives, our own happiness, our own success, Jesus, in John's gospel, reminds us that all our efforts will be vain unless they are made fruitful by the Father's gift, the gift of his love revealed in Jesus. A gift to be prayed for, 'Give me a drink'; a gift to be received, not fabricated: 'Everything is gift.'

To the Samaritan woman, Jesus offers the gift of 'living water': he had asked her: 'Give me a drink', because he was thirsty. He now offers her to give her a drink, to quench a thirst that is in her, and that she does not even recognize, of which she is not even aware: thirst for security far beyond that given her by the well and all it symbolizes; thirst for a happiness far beyond the limited joys of a harsh life; thirst for a communion far beyond the limits of the Samaritan community; thirst for a freedom no longer threatened by fear. Thirst for God: 'You have made us for yourself, O God, and our hearts are restless until they rest in you' (St Augustine, *Confessions*).

But how should we understand the words, 'living water'? 'Water, living water, a spring of living water in us...', what do these expressions mean?

Further on in his gospel, John uses again the expression, 'living water', and in some way explains it: 'On the last day of the festival, the greatest day, Jesus stood there and cried out: If anyone is thirsty, let him come to me, let the man come and drink who believes in me. As Scripture says, from his heart shall flow fountains of living water... He was speaking of the Spirit which those who believed in him were to receive ' (John 7:37-39).

Thus, for John, 'living water',—the 'living water' of a stream (as opposed to the stagnant water of a pond)—symbolises the Spirit of God, the 'Person-Love', as Pope John Paul calls the Spirit (*Tertio Millennio Adveniente*, n. 44); the Spirit who gives us new birth, new life (John 3:5); the Spirit who constantly invites us to let love be our guide and make us free (John 3:8).

The water of Jacob's well gave a sense of security to the

Samaritan woman; the 'living water' Jesus offers her will open her life to the security of love: 'So we have known and believe the love that God has for us. God is love, and those who abide in love abide in God, and God abides in them' (I John 4:16).

The Woman's Response

'Give me some of that water' (4:15). She is not quite sure what Jesus means, but she trusts him enough now to know that he is not fooling her, and therefore, she takes a timid step forward, 'Give me some of that water.' Later, she will come to a much more decisive step: 'The woman put down her water jar, and hurried back to the town to tell the people: 'Come and see' (John 4:28).

The woman's gesture expresses more powerfully than her words what her encounter with Jesus has done for her, in her. Her water jar has not become useless; but she now realizes that Jesus alone can fulfil her deepest longings for happiness and security.

I must be willing to take this gospel story, and read it as the story of an encounter taking place now, in my own life: Jesus, meeting me, and speaking to me. I must watch for images, words, which strike me and taste them, 'chew them', as long as I find them tasty. And joining the Samaritan woman, I too will say, 'Lord, give me of that water.'

What matters is not Where, but Whom you worship

In a rather abrupt manner, the dialogue between Jesus and the woman of Samaria now shifts from the water of the well to the temple where the Samaritans gather for worship:

'The woman said to him, "Sir, I see that you are a prophet. Our ancestors worshipped on this mountain, but you say that the place where people must worship is in Jerusalem." Jesus said to her, "Woman, believe me, the hour is coming when you will worship the Father neither on this mountain nor in Jerusalem. You worship what you do not know; we worship what we know, for salvation is from the Jews. But the hour is coming, and is now here, when the true worshippers will worship the Father in spirit and truth, for the Father seeks such as these to worship him. God is spirit, and those who worship him must worship in spirit and truth' (John 4:19-24)

There are very good reasons to believe that Jesus' words to the woman about her marriage situation (John 4:16-18) are to be understood symbolically: the woman, in a way, stands for her people who, for centuries, have been living outside the Covenant made by God with his chosen people. The prophets compared their situation to a situation of adultery, because they worshipped idols, and thus broke the marriage bond which united them to God (see Hosea 2:4). The woman senses that Jesus' words echo those of the prophets, and therefore, she puts to him a question which was closely connected with the Covenant: the question of the place of worship. She wonders whether there will still be a place for the Samaritan temple on Mount Gerizim in the new world Jesus has begun to open up for her: 'We, the Samaritans, worship on this mountain; but you, Jews, say it is in Jerusalem one ought to worship' 'What do you say?'

Where should one Worship?

It was an important question for the woman and her people: the Samaritan temple was the sacred symbol of their identity, of their autonomy, of their security; to them, their temple was 'the Lord's temple.'

It is an important question for many people today too: places of worship continue to play a major role in the lives of believers; they are, therefore, often objects of conflict. We think, for instance of the Holy Sepulchre in Jerusalem and the uneasy cohabitation there of different Christian communities. We think of the Golden Temple in Amritsar, India and of the violent conflict that developed around it a few years ago.

It is, of course, not just the Temple itself, the building, that matters; but also the rites, and prayers, and devotions connected with the Temple. In our own lives, we can think of all the expressions of our relationship to God, to 'our' God; expressions which correspond to the image we have of God. We can think of our prayer habits, the names we give to God, our own personal rituals; the rituals we perform every day. And the sense of security they give us, the sense of fulfilment, the sense of having done our

duty. Our 'religion', the religion to which we cling because, in
some way, it is part of our identity.

Thus, the woman's question to Jesus, 'Where should one
worship?' was a basic, vital question for her, for her people. It is
for us, too.

Jesus' answer: not 'Where' but 'Whom'!```

'Jesus said to her, "Woman, believe me, the hour is coming when
you will worship the Father neither on this mountain nor in
Jerusalem. You worship what you do not know; we worship what
we know, for salvation is from the Jews. But the hour is coming,
and is now here, when the true worshippers will worship the
Father in spirit and truth, for the Father seeks such as these to
worship him. God is spirit, and those who worship him must
worship in spirit and truth'" (John 4:21-24)

Obviously, Jesus does not deny the importance, the necessity
of places of worship, though in John's gospel, he clearly senses
how fragile and ambiguous temples can be (see John 2:13-22).

But Jesus has a major point to make: what matters most is not
where people worship: 'neither on this mountain, nor in Jerusa-
lem' (John 4,21); and that is true of whatever a temple stands for,
or symbolizes.

What matters most is *whom* you worship: The Lord our God is
the one Lord. And thus, once again, Jesus invites the Samaritan
Woman 'to go beyond', towards 'greater things' (John 1:50); to
go beyond the satisfaction, the sense of fulfilment, the security
she finds in the Samaritan Temple. God is greater, infinitely
greater than any Temple, any ritual, any prayer habits. God, and
more precisely, the God revealed by Jesus: the Father (whose
name appears three times 3 times in four verses), Abba.

Now the name 'Abba-Father', of itself, calls to our minds, not
first of all of a place, but rather a 'relationship', a family, a home
as a network of relationships centred on, finding its source in 'the
Father.' And if 'Abba' is the name of the God Jesus has come to
reveal to the world, then the worship of Jesus' God will necessarily
have to express the relationship of intimacy, tenderness, compas-
sion implied in the name 'Abba.'

It will be 'worship in Spirit and Truth' (the words appear twice, in v. 21 and v. 24); worship 'in the Spirit of truth': the Spirit of Jesus given us 'to remind us of Jesus' teaching' (John 14:26); given us to teach us everything, 'to lead us to the complete truth' (John 16:13). The Spirit who, as Paul puts it, 'cries out in us, Abba-Father' (Gal 4:6); or, in the beautiful words of Ignatius of Antioch, 'the Spirit, living water whispering in me, Come to the Father' (*Letter to the Romans*).

We must let Jesus' words to the Samaritan woman come to us and challenge our own personal approach to worship. What is my 'temple', which symbolizes my relationship to God, and the ways in which I express it? 'Things' which are important to me,—and for good reasons—to which I cling, about which I can easily become aggressive, if I feel challenged about them. Things which give me a feeling of security? We tend to be very conservative in the way we pray, in the 'prayers' we say, in the rituals we have adopted for ourselves over the years. Jesus, through John's gospel tells us, 'what matters most is the God you worship; let the Spirit make you free from whatever smacks of fear, of anxiety in the way you worship. May the Spirit guide you towards a relationship with Abba filled with childlike, joyful, loving trust. When you pray, say 'Abba'.

6

The Mystery of the Kingdom
'Father, you have revealed these things to the little ones'
(*Matthew 11 and 12*)

'Come, follow me': discipleship is a journey; a journey with Jesus; a journey on which we 'abide' with Jesus, and learn from him how to 'fish for people', a journey on which Jesus offers us the 'living water' of the Spirit to quench our thirst, and invites us to join him in saying, 'Abba-Father'.

Yet, it is by no means an easy road. It did lead Jesus to the triumph of Easter, but it first went up to Calvary. The gospels, especially perhaps Mark's and Matthew's, seem to highlight two major types of difficulties the disciples are bound to encounter on their journey: there are difficulties due to the radical demands of the gospel, demands from which people so often seek to escape. There are also difficulties coming from the disciples themselves; from their hearts. We will ask Matthew to guide us in our reflections on the first type of difficulties.

The Context – Matthew chapters 11-12

It is practically impossible to specify the exact historical context of the stories given us by the Evangelists about Jesus' ministry. Their aim is not to give us the historical development of that ministry but rather to offer us a catechesis based on Jesus' life and teaching. It might, however, be possible to outline at least some of the major articulations in the unfolding of Jesus' ministry.

The gospels seem to suggest that Jesus, the teacher, the healer was, at first, quite successful in Galilee: people were full of praise for his teaching and for his healing power: 'Here is a teaching that is new, and with authority behind it: he gives orders even to unclean spirits and they obey him.' And his reputation at once spread everywhere, through all the surrounding Galilean countryside' (Mark 1:27-28).

And yet, at the same time, people found it difficult to accept the challenge he offered them. He taught with authority, and people admired his teaching, but a number of them, afraid of the demands it made on them, were content with listening. He was a great healer, and that was wonderful; people applauded, and gave praise to God, but they could feel that Jesus' healing miracles contained a call to conversion which they were not prepared to accept. As to Jesus' freedom before the law, if again people loved to see the authority of their leaders challenged, it was bound to irritate the religious leaders themselves. To them, Jesus' freedom endangered the very fidelity of the Jewish community to God's Law.

The disciples must have enjoyed their Master's popularity: in some way they benefited by it; but they could not but sense, little by little, the growing of a certain passivity or indifference among the people, and of open opposition among the leaders. Chapters 11 and 12 seem to reflect this evolution. What is the role of these chapters in the first gospel?

Matthew opened his story of Jesus' ministry with the 'Sermon on the Mount' (chapters 5 to 7) which we can consider as 'the Charter of the Kingdom of Heaven.' The Evangelist has grouped together in this first long discourse of Jesus' the teaching which he considered as the very foundation of discipleship.

The following section of the gospel (8-10) could be entitled 'The Kingdom of Heaven in the making': chapters 8 and 9 group ten miracle stories, nine of which are stories of healing miracles. One already feels, however, in these two chapters, the beginning of some resistance, especially on the part of religious leaders who object to the liberty Jesus takes with the Law and Jewish traditions (9:1-17).

The apostolic discourse (chapter 10) in which Matthew has grouped sayings of Jesus for the use of Christian missionaries, stresses above all the difficulties which the disciples will meet as they are about to be sent on their first mission: 'Do not think that I have come to bring peace to the earth; I have not come to bring peace, but a sword. For I have come to set a man against his father, and a daughter against her mother, and a daughter-in-law against her mother-in-law' (Matthew 10:34-35).

My impression is that in chapters 11 and 12, Matthew wants to invite us to pause, to look back, and to evaluate the first part of Jesus' ministry in Galilee, perhaps in order to help us to be realistic, and at the same time, hopeful. The Jerusalem Bible entitles this new section, 'the Mystery of the Kingdom'.

The Mystery of the Kingdom of Heaven (Matthew 11 and 12)

Speaking after Pentecost to a pagan family in Caesarea, Peter summed up Jesus' ministry in these words: 'You know the message God sent to the people of Israel, preaching peace by Jesus Christ—he is Lord of all. That message spread throughout Judea, beginning in Galilee after the baptism that John announced: how God anointed Jesus of Nazareth with the Holy Spirit and with power; how he went about doing good and healing all who were oppressed by the devil, for God was with him' (Acts 10:36-38).

We could take it for granted that such a ministry of kindness and mercy could not but be welcomed and understood by all. But it was not so. Why? Matthew shows us how individuals or groups, in Galilee actually responded to Jesus.

John the Baptist and Jesus (Matthew 11:2-6)

Matthew begins with someone who evidently, we should think, was ready to understand Jesus, and to be filled with praise for his ministry: John the Baptist. This is how Matthew presents John's reaction to Jesus: 'When John heard in prison what the Messiah was doing, he sent word by his disciples and said to him, "Are you the one who is to come, or are we to wait for another?"' (11:2-3).

John had met Jesus near the Jordan, and had baptized him; and after his baptism, Jesus had spent some time with John (4:12), seemingly sharing in his ministry. The two men, therefore, must have known each other quite well. Matthew has already told us that John sensed that Jesus could be 'the one who was to come', 'the Messiah' (3:11). But how did John imagine the Messiah? Judging from what Matthew tells us about John's messianic expectations, John, expected the Messiah programmed by the

Scriptures, by the readers of the Scriptures, by the people who explained the Scriptures to the people: a Messiah sent by God to free Israel from its enemies, usher in the Day of God's retribution, punish sinners, reward the just, and restore the covenant community (3:1-10). The hope and dream shared by Jesus' contemporaries, and by the disciples!

But the reality of Jesus' ministry did not correspond to these hopes and dreams: 'Jesus went about all the cities and villages, teaching in their synagogues, and proclaiming the good news of the kingdom, and curing every disease and every sickness (9:35).

Hence the honest, simple, but also anxious question put to Jesus by John the Baptist: 'Are you the one who is to come or should we wait for another?' (11:3). A question which, however, actually challenged the whole of Jesus' ministry as if John wanted to say to him: 'what you are doing is good, but are you sure that it is what you should be doing?' In some way, John, and many of his contemporaries had the Messiah 'programmed', but Jesus simply did not fit in into their programme. We can easily sympathize with John the Baptist: it is so natural to us to seek to 'programme' everything: our lives, people, situations, and even God. In some way, we often behave as if 'reality' had to adapt to our expectations; as if God had to adapt to our dreams, and prayers. There might be very little room for adoration in our attitude to God, to 'the mystery of the Kingdom of Heaven.'

Jesus' answer to John's question was very clear: 'Go and tell John what you hear and see: the blind receive their sight, the lame walk, the lepers are cleansed, the deaf hear, the dead are raised, and the poor have good news brought to them. And blessed is anyone who takes no offence at me' (11:4-6).

In other words, behind Jesus' ministry, inspiring him, there was the immense freedom of God's love; and therefore, it was John who was invited to adapt his mind and heart to the reality of Jesus' ministry. John had to let the Spirit who guided Jesus transform him.

According to John the Evangelist, John the Baptist' response to Jesus' invitation was a wholehearted 'yes': 'He who has the bride is the bridegroom. The friend of the bridegroom, who stands and hears him, rejoices greatly at the bridegroom's voice.

For this reason my joy has been fulfilled. He must increase, but I must decrease' (John 3:29-30).

One could hardly imagine a better way of summing up what the journey of discipleship is about.

'This generation...' and Jesus (Matthew 11:16-19)

If John the Baptist found it difficult to understand Jesus' approach to his messianic ministry, what did people at large think? The people whom Jesus calls 'this generation'? 'To what will I compare this generation? It is like children sitting in the marketplaces'... For John came neither eating nor drinking, and they say, "He has a demon"; the Son of Man came eating and drinking, and they say, "Look, a glutton and a drunkard, a friend of tax collectors and sinners!" Yet wisdom is vindicated by her deeds" (11:16-19).

The expression, 'this generation', occurs several times in chapter 12, and it is always rather 'negative': perhaps it refers to a majority among Jesus' contemporaries. In our text, 'this generation' does not seem to be willing to accept Jesus.

Jesus compares it to children in the market place who would like to play but who cannot agree on the game they are going to play. They, therefore remain idle, shouting abuse at one another. In a similar manner, 'this generation' refused to pay heed to the message of the very austere John the Baptist: it decided he was mad! And now that Jesus of Nazareth has come, mixing with all sorts of people, and taking part in their feasts, 'this generation' rejects him for being 'a glutton and a drunkard.'

'This generation' was sick of a very common 'illness': it did not want to be challenged, it did not want to get involved in anything serious. Its favourite weapon was to criticize whatever or whoever could disturb them: putting labels, negative labels on people was for them an excellent substitute for change. 'This generation' is very much alive today; actually, it has a foothold in our own hearts; in my own heart.

The Lake-Towns and Jesus (Matthew 11:20-24)

Among the people who must have been most familiar with Jesus, the lake-towns had a privileged place: Chorazin, Bethsaida, and especially Capernaum, the town where Jesus had his house (see Mark 9:33).

What was their attitude to Jesus? 'Then he began to reproach the cities in which most of his deeds of power had been done, because they did not repent. "Woe to you, Chorazin! Woe to you, Bethsaida! And you, Capernaum..."' (11:20).

There seems to be sadness in Matthew's remark: the cities 'in which most of his deeds of power had been done'... The people, in these towns, ought to have been deeply touched by Jesus' immense concern and compassion for the sick, for marginalised. Instead, what seems to have struck them was the 'power' displayed in Jesus' miracles; and they had become 'miracle-addicts' asking for signs, for more signs, signs out of the ordinary; but unable, perhaps, to understand that Jesus wanted them to be themselves signs to people—they had to be God's hands, and eyes, and heart in the world. Witnesses of Jesus' healing miracles, they would not join Jesus in his ministry of compassion.

The Pharisees

The Pharisees occupy the centre stage in Matthew chapter 12. Who were they, what was their role in the community of God's People?

They were the spiritual leaders of the Jewish community: serious, zealous, learned people, their major concern was fidelity to the covenant community to the covenant Law. It was in the light of the Law that they tended to judge, to evaluate situations and people.

Jesus' freedom before the Law irritated and scandalised them. To them, obeying the Law literally took precedence over everything else; they had no objection to Jesus healing the sick, provided it was not on the Sabbath (Mark 3:1-6). Jesus' attitude threatened the security they found in the Law. They came to the point where they wondered whether Jesus was not inspired by Satan!

'Then they brought to him a demoniac who was blind and mute; and he cured him, so that the one who had been mute could speak and see. All the crowds were amazed and said, "Can this be the Son of David?" But when the Pharisees heard it, they said, "It is only by Beelzebul, the ruler of the demons, that this fellow casts out the demons"' (Matthew 12:22-24)

This is a temptation which might be present in some way or other in the ministry of religious leaders. While admitting that the wind blows where it wills, they may find it very difficult to accept that law, discipline and order are for people, and that therefore people must be given priority. The danger, for the Pharisees, was that they might come to the point where they would say 'no' to the light (the sin against the Spirit: Matthew 12:31-32).

Do the severe warnings Jesus gives to the Pharisees concern us, concern me? Whenever we come across a text in the gospels in which the Pharisees oppose Jesus, in which Jesus reproaches the Pharisees for their attitude, we may very easily think that the Pharisees today are, of course, those people over there. The truth is that there is a Pharisee in each one of us: a Pharisee who is lord and master in areas in which I am sure I know best, in which I sit in judgement over people, or situations—areas in which I am not just serious, but intolerant; and therefore deaf to the call of the gospel.

Jesus' Family (Matthew 12:46-50)

'While he was still speaking to the crowds, his mother and his brothers were standing outside, wanting to speak to him. Someone told him, "Look, your mother and your brothers are standing outside, wanting to speak to you." But to the one who had told him this, Jesus replied, "Who is my mother, and who are my brothers?" And pointing to his disciples, he said, "Here are my mother and my brothers! For whoever does the will of my Father in heaven is my brother and sister and mother"' (12:46-50)

Jesus' attitude to his family as shown in this text, may appear harsh to us. We must remember, however, that the Jewish family in Jesus' time formed a closely knit community on whose fidelity all members could count, especially in times of trouble, but to whom all members had to be ready to give priority in their relationships. Jesus' family was no exception. But Jesus constantly

refused to have his family interfering in any way with his ministry. To him, family ties were decided by fidelity to the word of
God; no one was excluded; his family, the family which his ministry aimed at bringing together, was as wide as faithfulness to
God. As wide as God's love.

Being 'possessive' is another common human illness: we can so
easily be possessive of people, even possessive of God, of God's bless-
ings, of the Church...! The way Jonah was: he simply would not believe that God could love the pagans of Niniveh: it took him a three-
day retreat in the belly of a whale to begin to understand that God's
concern extends to every single living being (Jonah 4:9-11).

If we now look back on Matthew chapters 11 and 12, we must
admit that the picture given us in these chapters by the Evangelist of the first part of Jesus' ministry in Galilee is very dark indeed: John the Baptist doubted, 'this generation' refused to get
involved; the lake towns refused to repent; the Pharisees objected
to Jesus and his teaching; Jesus' family did not understand him.
We can easily guess how the disciples must have felt as they were
becoming more and more aware of what was going on.

Can we find a common denominator to all these negative
attitudes encountered by Jesus? Perhaps we could say that the
basic problem for people was the expectations they had concerning the Messiah: in some way or other, they all had the Messiah programmed, and because Jesus did not fit in with their
programme, some of them doubted, others objected, most of
them tried to escape from the demands of the gospel.

It is important for us to realise that all these people are, in
some way, in us; their difficulties can easily be ours. Reality often frightens us, even the reality of God makes us feel ill-at-ease
; and we instinctively try to bend it to suit our desires, our programme; and if we cannot, we try to escape. Matthew, therefore,
also speaks to us.

Jesus and the Mystery of the Kingdom

How did Jesus' react? What did he feel when he looked at the
way people responded, or rather, failed to respond to his ministry?

Jesus himself seems to answer our question in a text which we must consider as the very core of the gospel: 'At that time Jesus said, "I thank you, Father, Lord of heaven and earth, because you have hidden these things from the wise and the intelligent and have revealed them to infants; yes, Father, for such was your gracious will. All things have been handed over to me by my Father; and no one knows the Son except the Father, and no one knows the Father except the Son and anyone to whom the Son chooses to reveal him. "Come to me, all you that are weary and are carrying heavy burdens, and I will give you rest"' (Matthew 11:25-30)

In Matthew's gospel, as we read it today, we find this text at the very end of chapter 11; we could say that it is like a hinge between chapters 11 and 12. In other words, while John the Baptist doubts, while 'this generation' refuses to commit itself, while the lake towns refuse to repent, while the Pharisees object, and while Jesus' family does not understand him, Jesus expresses his joyful praise to the Father: 'I thank you, Father...'

What is the cause of Jesus' joyful praise?

The Message of the Text

This is how C.H. Dodd [1] sums it up : 'At the heart of the storm there was a centre of calm: "No one knows the Son but the Father; and no one knows the Father but the Son."' In the gospel according to John this theme of the mutual 'knowledge' of Father and Son is developed in theological terms; and indeed there is a whole theology implicit in it. But in the saying as I have quoted it from Matthew (and Luke has it with slight verbal differences) is not theology but a spontaneous personal statement. It begins with a confession of the deep loneliness which was increasingly the lot of Jesus; he has found no one who really knows or understands him, not even those nearest to him; but there is one who does know him—God, his Father. And in that same intimate, personal way he too knows God. Here, we may legitimately infer, is to be found the driving force and the source of energy for an almost impossible mission; here certainly the

---

1. C. H. Dodd, *Founder of Christianity*, London, Fontana Books, p 63

source of the inflexible resolution with which he knowingly wen to death in the service of his mission. The words of the Fourth Gospel here ring true: 'It is meat and drink for me to do the will of him who sent me until I have finished his work'; and according to the same gospel he moved into the final loneliness of his friendless death with the words, as simple as they could well be, 'I am not alone, because the Father is with me.'

Thus, in a context of crisis, Jesus expresses his joy and praises the Father. He is not naive, he is aware of the way people react to his ministry; he knows that 'the learned and the clever' do not understand him, refuse to accept him and his message, refuse to respond to his call; in Matthew's context, 'the learned and the clever' might be especially the Pharisees of chapter 12.

But that is only part of the picture: Jesus is equally aware of how the poor, the little ones do respond; they seemed to be attuned to the gospel. Who were the little ones for Jesus? In all likelihood, they were the poor who did not know much about the Law; sinners, the marginalised, whom Jewish society despised because they lived outside the Law; the people whom Jesus welcomed and who often were his table-companions.

These were people who were aware of their own poverty, and longed for liberation, for salvation, for communion, for forgiveness. They, therefore, flocked to Jesus because they sensed that he loved them; they grasped his message, they welcomed the 'revelation' which his ministry offered them; the revelation of a God who was 'Father - Abba', a God of immense kindness and mercy. Not the God of the Pharisees, but the God of Jesus. In and through Jesus, they began to discover the face of God.

And that revelation touched their hearts, their lives. They now knew that whatever happened, whatever the condemnation uttered against them by those who knew, who were clever, God was near, inviting them to draw near, to entrust their burden to him: '"Come to me, all you that are weary and are carrying heavy burdens, and I will give you rest. Take my yoke upon you, and learn from me; for I am gentle and humble in heart, and you will find rest for your souls. For my yoke is easy, and my burden is light.' (Matthew 11:28-30). The relief, the joy it was for them;

the joy of the *Magnificat.*

Commenting on the use of the word, 'conversion-repentance' in the Gospels, Joachim Jeremias, a New Testament theologian, writes: 'Repentance means learning to say "Abba" again' [2]

Matthew chapters 11 and 12 are evidently, for us, an invitation to conversion, to change; an invitation to become like infants, like the little ones who gave so much joy to Jesus; they found it so easy, so natural, to say 'Abba' to the God of Jesus; they felt at home with the God revealed by Jesus. To us who so often behave like 'the learned and the clever', and love to programme everything, God included, the point is of course not simply to call God 'Abba', but to let go into Abba's hands; to let Jesus, our way to Abba, grow greater in us, while we ourselves grow smaller.

Growing smaller is a battle. It is good to hear Jesus telling us: 'Come to me, all you who labour and are overburdened, and I will give you rest.'

7

The Servant's Journey
'On the road to Jerusalem'
(Mark 8 to 10)

Called to follow Jesus, the disciples found it difficult to accept the way Jesus' ministry was unfolding: 'the learned and the clever', among whom were many influential people, did not understand Jesus, they did not respond to his challenge; a number of them openly objected to Jesus' message. And that could lead to disaster: a fate which no one, in Jesus' time, would have ever associated with the Messiah's mission.

But there was more. There was, in the disciples, as there in us, a longing for power and for all the paraphernalia which so often accompany it, which is incompatible with the gospel. Perhaps we could say that for Jesus, power (and money: power and money so often go together!) was a major obstacle on the journey of discipleship. That seems to be the focus of a rich and interesting catechesis found in Mark's gospel, chapters 8 to 10.

The Context: the Loaves (Mark 6:30-52)

In order to understand Mark's catechesis, we must go back to the story of the multiplication of the loaves. Let us note first the conclusion of that story: 'So they sat down in groups of hundreds and of fifties. Taking the five loaves and the two fish, he looked up to heaven, and blessed and broke the loaves, and gave them to his disciples to set before the people; and he divided the two fish among them all. And all ate and were filled; and they took up twelve baskets full of broken pieces and of the fish. Those who had eaten the loaves numbered five thousand men' (Mark 6:40-44)

The multiplication of loaves was an important event in Jesus' Galilean ministry; so important that we have six stories of it (two in Mark, two in Matthew, one in Luke, one in John). But why was it considered as particularly important? Perhaps, first of all, because of the magnitude of the experience: Jesus had given a very abundant meal to such a big crowd of people. There was also the link which the very first Christian communities seem to have seen between the loaves and the Lord's Supper as they celebrated it. Actually, the gesture of Jesus blessing the loaves and having them distributed is described with words which may very well have been part of the ritual of the 'Breaking of Bread' in the early Church: 'Taking the five loaves... Jesus looked up to heaven, and blessed and broke the loaves and gave them to the disciples...'

But whatever the importance attached to the episode of the loaves, we are struck by the fact that in spite of the magnitude of the miracle, Mark does not tell us anything about the crowd's reaction. He simply concludes his story with the words: 'Those who had eaten the loaves numbered five thousand men.'

Not only that, but Mark goes on to tell us that Jesus, immediately after the loaves, obliged the disciples to get into a boat, and to go ahead of him to Bethsaida. Should we therefore understand that the disciples did not want to go, and Jesus had to force them? But why was Jesus so insistent that the disciples should go away immediately?

After the disciples had left, Jesus sent the crowd away, and later, during the night, he walked on the lake in order to join the disciples who found it difficult to make headway because the wind was against them. And this is how Mark concludes his story of Jesus on the lake: 'Then he got into the boat with them and the wind ceased. And they were utterly astounded, for they did not understand about the loaves, but their hearts were hardened' (6:51-52)

'They did not understand about the loaves but their hearts were hardened': what was it that the disciples had failed to grasp about the loaves? Mark does not say.

Perhaps, however, we do find an answer to our questions in the conclusion of John's story of the loaves: 'When the people saw the sign that he had done, they began to say, "This is indeed the prophet who is to come into the world." When Jesus realized that they were about to come and take him by force to make him king, he withdrew again to the mountain by himself' (John 6:14-15).

Thus, according to John, the response given to Jesus by the crowds (and by the disciples) to the feast he had offered them was political: they meant 'to come and take him by force to make him king'. 'If Jesus had been a Messiah of the common sort, it was a golden opportunity; but that sort of messiahship he had rejected long ago as a temptation of the devil.'[1] The disciples could not understand or accept Jesus' reaction.

In other words, we have reasons to believe that the episode of the loaves marked the beginning of a crisis between Jesus and his disciples; and it seems to have led Jesus to take several important decisions: he must soon leave Galilee, in order to go to Jerusalem, and there confront Judaism at the very heart of its institutions. He must also give more time to the disciples: they still have such a long way to go in order to understand his message. And therefore he will now leave the lake shore and go to the coast (Tyre and Sidon), and to the north (Caesarea Philippi), at the foot of Mount Hermon... away from the crowds (Mark 9:30-31).

It was this crisis and its consequences for Jesus and for the disciples that Mark seems to have used in order to give us a catechesis on the journey of discipleship.

Journey — the Central Theme of Mark's Catechesis

It is clearly and often underlined. 'On the way, he put this question to his disciples' (8:27). 'What were you arguing about on the road? (9:30,33). 'They were on the road, going up to Jerusalem, Jesus was walking on ahead of them' (10:32).

What does Mark want to tell us? Perhaps he wants to draw our attention to the fact that discipleship is actually a journey, an experience which takes time to unfold, to mature; a journey which, actually, is as long as life itself. It is also a difficult journey: there are plenty of obstacles on the way; at times we go forward, at times backward; we encounter risks, dangers; we experience successes but also failures; the road itself is more often than not, a bush path.

---

1. C.H.Dodd, *The Founder of Christianity*, London: Fontana Books 1973, p 141-142)

But whatever the difficulties, the obstacles, the journey of discipleship is always a 'journey with Jesus'; Jesus whom the evangelists often show walking ahead; a journey on which, in the words of the Letter to the Hebrews, 'we must never lose sight of Jesus who leads us in our faith and brings it to perfection' (Hebrews 12:2).

On the Way to Jerusalem with Jesus

Mark highlights what I call three 'moments' in this journey; three 'moments' which show us the disciples in conflict with Jesus; there does not seem to be any progress, from one moment to another, in the disciples' attitude. The only progress is that of the journey itself which takes Jesus and his disciples from Caesarea Philippi, at the foot of Mount Hermon, in northern Galilee, to Capernaum on the northwest shore of the Lake of Galilee, to Jericho, in the south, a few miles from Jerusalem.

Caesarea Philippi: 'Who do you say I am?'

'Jesus went on with his disciples to the villages of Caesarea Philippi; and on the way he asked his disciples, "Who do people say that I am?" And they answered him, "John the Baptist; and others, Elijah; and still others, one of the prophets." He asked them, "But who do you say that I am?" Peter answered him, "You are the Messiah." And he sternly ordered them not to tell anyone about him. Then he began to teach them that the Son of Man must undergo great suffering, and be rejected by the elders, the chief priests, and the scribes, and be killed, and after three days rise again. He said all this quite openly. And Peter took him aside and began to rebuke him. But turning and looking at his disciples, he rebuked Peter and said, "Get behind me, Satan! For you are setting your mind not on divine things but on human things." He called the crowd with his disciples, and said to them, "If any want to become my followers, let them deny themselves and take up their cross and follow me"' (Mark 8:27-34).

According to Mark's story, Jesus, after the episode of the loaves, left the lake shore and went first to the coast in the region of Tyre and Sidon (7:24), and then later further north, to Caesarea Philippi. As Mark will put it later, 'He did not want anyone to know it; for he was teaching his disciples' (9:31).

They obviously had still much to learn: they were still at the stage where the Jesus they followed was more the Jesus-Messiah of their imagination, of their ambitions, than the real Jesus. The two questions put to them by Jesus were an invitation given them to assess the place he really had in their lives: 'Who do people say I am, Who do you say I am?' For men and women called to 'follow' Jesus, to abide with him, it was, it remains, the most fundamental question.

The first question, 'who do people say...?' , was an easy one. It was directed to the disciples' memory; whatever other people can say does not really touch the core of my life. The disciples were, therefore, able to report at least some of the opinions they had heard voiced by people: 'John the Baptist; and others, Elijah; and still others, one of the prophets.'

Jesus' second question was much more challenging: 'who do *you* say I am?...' It was a question put, not just to the mind or the memory of the disciples, but to their heart.

Peter's answer was immediate; too immediate perhaps to have much depth: 'You are the Christ'! In Matthew's gospel, Peter's crisp answer is followed by a solemn, post-Easter profession of faith: 'You are the Christ, the Son of the Living God'; and Jesus congratulates Peter on the gift granted to him by the Father: 'Simon, son of Jonah, you are a blessed man! And Jesus answered him, "Blessed are you, Simon son of Jonah! For flesh and blood has not revealed this to you, but my Father in heaven. And I tell you, you are Peter, and on this rock I will build my church, and the gates of Hades will not prevail against it. I will give you the keys of the kingdom of heaven, and whatever you bind on earth will be bound in heaven, and whatever you loose on earth will be loosed in heaven' (Matthew 16:17-19).

In Mark, we have instead, a severe warning from Jesus; 'And he sternly ordered them not to tell anyone about him (8:30). Why this severity of Jesus? Surely, there was truth in Peter's answer: 'You are the Christ'; it was, so to speak, a first step in the right direction. Though, of course, much depended on what the title 'Messiah-Christ' meant for Peter and the other disciples.

Jesus, however, did not want his Messiahship to be proclaimed just now; he was fully aware of the ambiguity of the word 'Messiah'; it was associated, in the minds of people, in the disciples' minds, with images of power and riches. In Mark's gospel, it will only be at the beginning of his Passion, after his arrest that, interrogated by the Jewish authorities, he will acknowledge his messiahship: 'The high priest asked him, "Are you the Messiah, the Son of the Blessed One?" Jesus said, "I am; and you will see the Son of Man seated at the right hand of the Power, and coming with the clouds of heaven"' (14:61-62).

But at Caesarea Philippi, Jesus must share with his disciples his own understanding of his mission as the Messiah. In so doing, he avoids even the word 'Messiah' and uses the much prosaic title of 'Son of Man': the Son of Man who, one day, it is true, will be seated at the right hand of God', but who now, is 'son of man', 'in all things like us but sin'; a son of man on his way to Jerusalem, where he will confront Judaism at the very seat of its power. And even at this stage in his ministry, Jesus knows enough about the history of his people to understand that Jerusalem could very well mean for him suffering, rejection, failure, death, though he is sure, even now, of God's final victory, the victory of life.

The shock Jesus' words gave the disciples is expressed by Peter: 'And Peter took Jesus aside and began to rebuke him.' In Peter's understanding of the Messiah, there was no room for failure, for suffering, or for death. Sent by God, the Messiah could not but be a winner!

Peter's understanding of Jesus' messiahship was in some way that of all disciples: instinctively, so to speak, we see God, and God's Messiah as invested with power, a power which no force can possibly curb. To the disciples in the gospels, this understanding of Jesus' Messiahship was vital for them, because they felt that in some way, their fate was linked with his.

Jesus' reaction to Peter was severe: 'Turning and looking at his disciples, he rebuked Peter and said, "Get behind me, Satan! For you are setting your mind not on divine things but on human things" (8:33).

These words of Jesus to Peter are found even in Matthew's version of Caesarea Philippi: Peter is the rock on which the Church is founded, he can also be Satan to Jesus himself (Matthew 16:23).

This warning of Jesus is given, not just to Peter, but to all disciples: 'He called the crowd with his disciples, and said to them, "If any want to become my followers, let them deny themselves and take up their cross and follow me. For those who want to save their life will lose it, and those who lose their life for my sake, and for the sake of the gospel, will save it. For what will it profit them to gain the whole world and forfeit their life? Indeed, what can they give in return for their life? ' (Mark 8:34-37)

Thus, for Jesus, what comes first is *life*: we want to live, to live fully, to fulfil our tremendous zest for life. We are quite right: that is what God wants for us, God whose glory, in the words of St Irenaeus, is 'a human being fully alive.' But the way to an always fuller life is not that of power but of love, that is the way of self-denial. The way followed by Jesus.

Capernaum: '...last of all and servant of all'

'They went on from there and passed through Galilee. He did not want anyone to know it; for he was teaching his disciples, saying to them, "The Son of Man is to be betrayed into human hands, and they will kill him, and three days after being killed, he will rise again." But they did not understand what he was saying and were afraid to ask him.

'Then they came to Capernaum; and when he was in the house he asked them, "What were you arguing about on the way?" But they were silent, for on the way they had argued with one another who was the greatest. He sat down, called the twelve, and said to them, "Whoever wants to be first must be last of all and servant of all." Then he took a little child and put it among them; and taking it in his arms, he said to them, "Whoever welcomes one such child in my name welcomes me, and whoever welcomes me welcomes not me but the one who sent me"' (Mark 9:30-37)

'On the way': the journey towards Jerusalem continues. So does, of course, 'the journey of discipleship'; a journey on which

Jesus walks ahead of his disciples, showing them the way.

And for the second time, Jesus reminds them that the road on which he leads them goes to Jerusalem, that is, to his Passion, 'for he was teaching his disciples, saying to them, "The Son of Man is to be betrayed into human hands, and they will kill him, and three days after being killed, he will rise again"' (Mark 9:31).

But, as Mark points out, 'They did not understand what he was saying, and were afraid to ask him'. They understood so little that, 'on the way', they had a heated discussion on a question which, to them, was of great importance: 'Who was the greatest?' It was childish on their part; and they felt ashamed of themselves when Jesus asked them: 'What were you arguing about on the road' (9:33).

Jesus, however, patiently tried to help them accept the reality of his mission: the discussion they had had showed how ambitious they all were. And Jesus, in some way, encouraged them to be ambitious, to be even much more ambitious: 'set your hearts on the more important gifts', as Paul will write to the Christians of Corinth (I Corinthians 12:31). Jesus even gave them an infallible recipe for success: 'Whoever wants to be first must be last of all and servant of all.' And if they needed a visual aid to grasp what it really meant, it was enough for them to think of small children: 'Then he took a little child and put it among them; and taking it in his arms, he said to them, it is to such as these that the kingdom of God belongs' (Mark 9:36 and 10:15). 'A little child', that is, someone able to say spontaneously to God, in loving trust, as Jesus did: 'Abba'.

Jericho: '...like the Son of Man who came to serve'

'They were on the road, going up to Jerusalem, and Jesus was walking ahead of them; they were amazed, and those who followed were afraid. He took the twelve aside again and began to tell them what was to happen to him, saying, "See, we are going up to Jerusalem, and the Son of Man will be handed over to the chief priests and the scribes, and they will condemn him to death; then they will hand him over to the Gentiles; they will mock him, and spit upon him, and flog him, and kill him; and after three days he will rise again."

'James and John, the sons of Zebedee, came forward to him and said to him, "Teacher, we want you to do for us whatever we ask of you." And he said to them, "What is it you want me to do for you?" And they said to him, "Grant us to sit, one at your right hand and one at your left, in your glory."

'When the ten heard this, they began to be angry with James and John. So Jesus called them and said to them, "You know that among the Gentiles those whom they recognize as their rulers lord it over them, and their great ones are tyrants over them. But it is not so among you; but whoever wishes to become great among you must be your servant, and whoever wishes to be first among you must be slave of all. For the Son of Man came not to be served but to serve, and to give his life a ransom for many"' (Mark 10:32-45).

Jesus and his disciples had now reached Jericho, a few miles from Jerusalem; the disciples' mood was one of darkness, of apprehension. They realised how serious Jesus had been when, near Caesarea Philippi, he had, for the first time, announced his intention to go to Jerusalem, whatever the cost. Jesus' words now could not but increase their fears: 'See, we are going up to Jerusalem, and the Son of Man will be handed over to the chief priests and the scribes, and they will condemn him to death; then they will hand him over to the Gentiles; they will mock him, and spit upon him, and flog him, and kill him; and after three days he will rise again' (Mark 10:33-34).

We are, therefore, shocked when we see James and John approaching Jesus and asking him to grant them the first two places in the Kingdom: 'Allow us to sit one at your right hand and the other at your left in your glory'! That actually sounded so unbelievable to Matthew that, in his own story, he has, instead of James and John, Mrs Zebedee, their mother, go to Jesus and present their request to him. We have enough personal experience of how blind ambition can make us understand that the two men did not need their mother to act on their behalf.

The two men's request obviously showed complete misunderstanding of Jesus, and a total lack of sensitivity for his feelings; they were inspired by an unbridled ambition, which was shared by the other disciples: 'When the other ten heard this they began to feel indignant' (Mark 10:41).

And so, once again, Jesus, patiently tried to help his disciples face the reality of discipleship: 'You know that among the Gentiles those whom they recognize as their rulers lord it over them, and their great ones are tyrants over them. But it is not so among you; whoever wishes to become great among you must be your servant, and whoever wishes to be first among you must be slave of all. For the Son of Man came not to be served but to serve, and to give his life a ransom for many.'

There are two possible types of relationships between us: we can behave like 'pagans', that is, lord it over people, and make our authority felt; and we know what that means, because we have already experienced it, and we probably have made other people experience it. But instead, as disciples of Jesus, we should seek to be 'servants', and 'slaves to all.' Like the Son of Man who came, not be served, but to serve, and to give his life as a ransom for many', that is, in order to bring freedom to the people.

If we wanted to sum up the teaching Jesus gave his disciples as they were making their way towards Jerusalem and the Passion, one word might suffice: Jesus' way was that of a 'servant', it must also be the disciples' way: to serve, out of love. A way, a road on which there is, usually, very little competition. The road which the celebration of the Eucharist invites us to follow: Jesus, 'bread broken and shared for the life of the world', telling us, 'Do this in memory of me.'

'Lord, that I may see'

In the stories on which we have just been reflecting, we have found expressed two radically opposed visions of life: that of Jesus, and that of the disciples. Because he wanted to reveal Abba to the world, Jesus chose to be 'the man for others'; and one word sums up his vision, 'service', loving service. The disciples' dream could also be summed up in one word: power, and no doubt, power accompanied by all its trimmings.

Could we, should we say that our own dreams today are very

much the same as that of Jesus' disciples? In case we would hesitate to admit it, Mark wants us to realise how easily we can fool ourselves, simply because we are blind.

Mark actually prefaces and concludes his catechesis on leadership in the Christian community with two stories of Jesus healing two blind people.

The Blind Man of Bethsaida

'(Jesus and his disciples) came to Bethsaida. Some people brought a blind man to him and begged him to touch him. He took the blind man by the hand and led him out of the village; and when he had put saliva on his eyes and laid his hands on him, he asked him, "Can you see anything?" And the man looked up and said, "I can see people, but they look like trees, walking." Then Jesus laid his hands on his eyes again; and he looked intently and his sight was restored, and he saw everything clearly. Then he sent him away to his home, saying, "Do not even go into the village"' (Mark 8:22-26).

The 'Bethsaida' of this story happens to have been the home of Peter, Andrew and Philip (John 1:44; 12:21). Perhaps there is here a significant coincidence. As to the blind man Jesus met there, he must have been afflicted with a particularly grave and resistant form of blindness since it took Jesus two attempts to heal him completely.

Placed as it is just before the episode of Caesarea Philippi (8:27-33), this story may be seen as a warning given by the Evangelist to the disciples of all times; and to us.

The Blind Man of Jericho

'They came to Jericho. As he and his disciples and a large crowd were leaving Jericho, Bartimaeus son of Timaeus, a blind beggar, was sitting by the roadside. When he heard that it was Jesus of Nazareth, he began to shout out and say, "Jesus, Son of David, have mercy on me!" Many sternly ordered him to be quiet, but he cried out even more loudly, "Son of David, have mercy on me!" Jesus stood still and said, "Call him here." And they called the blind man, saying to him, "Take heart; get up, he is calling you." So throwing off his cloak, he sprang up and came to Jesus. Then Jesus said to him, "What do you want me to do for you?" The blind man said to him, "My teacher, let me see again." Jesus said to him, "Go; your faith has made you well." Immediately he regained his sight and followed him on the way' (Mark 10:46-52).

Thus, Mark concludes his catechesis on the Journey of Discipleship as he had opened it, with the story of a blind man healed by Jesus. The question put by Jesus to Bartimaeus is basically the same as his question to James and John: 'What do you want me to do for you?' (Mark 10:36 and 51). But where James and John asked for the first two places in the Kingdom, Bartimaeus simply answers: 'My teacher, let me see again.'

The conclusion of Mark's story is remarkable: 'Immediately he regained his sight and followed him on the way' (10:52); Jesus' healing has given him the power to follow Jesus, that is, to be truly a disciple.

We can easily make our own Bartimaeus' prayer: 'Lord, that I may see!' That I may grow more and more aware of the thirst for power that is in me, and of the many ways in which I seek to assert my power over people, over things, over situations. I might do it 'gently', even perhaps with a certain elegance; but it is still seeking to be in control. And love is inevitably the loser.

Jesus invites me to follow him, and to give free rein to my ambition, provided it be directed towards 'serving lovingly': 'Whoever wants to be first must be last of all and servant of all.'

The Transfiguration
'This is my Son, listen to him'
(*Mark 9:2-8*)

The journey which took Jesus and his disciples from Galilee to Jerusalem was, especially according to Mark's gospel, difficult: Jesus' popularity seemed to have been on the wane, and the disciples could see their dreams of power lose ground before the harsh reality of a road which would bring them face to face with the religious authorities in the Holy City.

Was there any ray of hope which could bolster up their courage, renew their vision? The experience of Jesus' Transfiguration ought to have been just that for them: 'In God's light, they could have seen the light' (Psalm 36:9).

'Six days later...' The context of the Transfiguration in Jesus' ministry

The Transfiguration story is to be found in the gospels of Mark, Matthew and Luke; and the three evangelists place it at roughly the same moment in Jesus' ministry, that is, shortly after the episode of Caesarea Philippi (Mark 8:27-9:1 and 9:2-8).

Concretely, what does that mean? The episode of Caesarea Philippi marked, for Jesus and his disciples, the beginning of a dark night: as Mark puts it, it was then that Jesus began 'to teach them that the Son of Man was destined to suffer grievously... And he said this quite openly' (Mark 8:31-32).

We know, from Mark's gospel, the shock Jesus' words were for the disciples; the shock voiced by Peter, 'Peter started to remonstrate with him' (Mark 8:32).

Jesus' reaction to Peter is among the harshest in the gospels: 'Get behind me, Satan, because the way you think is not God's, but man's' (Mark 8:33). It was a clash between God's way and man's way; between the political messianism which the disciples

of all times may find so attractive, and the 'messianism.' Jesus
had in mind, the Servant's 'messianism'. The clash between Satan's vision and Abba's vision; the clash between a vision of victory through power and riches, and a vision where love is the
only reality that counts.

Thus, at Caesarea Philippi, the crisis provoked by the loaves
seems to have deepened. Both Jesus and his disciples entered
then a dark night: the disciples first because Jesus' words had
shattered their dreams. But it was darkness for Jesus too: he was
then about thirty and the prospect of suffering, of failure, and
perhaps of death, could not but affect him deeply. And there
was also his disciples' disarray: they could not understand him,
they could not really 'follow' him.

And it was then, 'six days later', as Mark puts it that Jesus
went up to a high mountain... (Mark 9:2-8).

The Experience of the Transfiguration

The Transfiguration story must not be read as if it were a video.
It is rather a story meant to express, with the help of symbols
familiar to readers of the Scriptures, an experience Jesus and
his three companions were given of God at a crucial moment in
Jesus' ministry, a crucial moment in the disciples' journey.

We could speak of a 'threshold', an experience which marked
the beginning of a new phase in Jesus' mission, the phase leading up to Jerusalem and the Passion.

A God-given Experience

Three main symbols bring out the God-givenness of the Transfiguration experience.

According to the gospels, it was Jesus who took the initiative
of going up a mountain with three of his companions: 'In most
religions, the mountains, probably because of their height and
the air of mystery which enshrouds them, are considered to be
the point where heaven and earth meet.'[1] Luke brings this out
when he writes: 'he went up to the mountain to pray. As he

1. *Dictionary of Biblical Theology.* London, Geoffrey Chapman 1973. 'Mountain', p 372

prayed, the aspect of his face was changed' (9:29).

As to the cloud which covered the disciples with shadow, it is, in the Old Testament, one of the privileged symbols of God's presence among his people, especially during their 'exodus' in the desert. It was 'in the cloud' that God accompanied his people; we could say that the 'cloud' was God's means of transport and testified to God's presence; but at the same time, it reminded the Israelites that God was beyond them; so near yet untouchable' (see Numbers 9:15-23).

It is, however, the voice from the cloud which is the major symbol in the story; it highlights the core of the Transfiguration experience: 'This is my Son'— a voice expressing kindness and mercy, concern, nearness.

An Experience of Light

The three Synoptic gospels stress that the Transfiguration experience was an experience of light:

Mark: 'There in their presence he was transfigured: his clothes became brilliantly white; whiter than any earthly bleacher could make them' (9:2-3).

Matthew: 'His face shone like the sun and his clothes became as dazzling as light' (17:2).

Luke: 'As he was praying, the aspect of his face was changed and his clothing became sparkling white' (9:29).

Thus it was God's light which was projected onto the dark night into which Jesus and his disciples had entered; a light which was focused on Jesus, and permeated his whole being. Jesus at this precise moment in his ministry: the Jesus of the Loaves; the Jesus of Caesarea Philippi; the Jesus speaking about his decision to go up to Jerusalem for his Passion, the Jesus speaking about his suffering, and death, and resurrection.

The Transfiguration experience was an experience of God meant to throw light onto the mystery of Jesus' person, of his mission. The presence of Moses and Elijah at Jesus' side confirms this interpretation. It expresses the continuity between their experience and Jesus': yes, this Jesus is truly the promised Messiah, but God's Messiah, the Father's Messiah.

The disciples were therefore invited to 'listen to Jesus'; invited to accept, to welcome Jesus just as he was; invited to be disciples of Jesus just as he was: the Jesus of miracles; Jesus the teacher whose authority impressed them and gave them such joy and hope; but also the Jesus of the loaves who refused political power; and the Jesus of Caesarea speaking about his going up to Jerusalem where he might have to suffer and die; and tomorrow, the Jesus of Gethsemane, the Jesus of Calvary, the Jesus of Easter.

The Transfiguration was, for the disciples, an invitation to surrender, to let go of their dreams about Jesus (and themselves) and to follow 'the real of Jesus': 'This is my Son, the Beloved, listen to him' (Mark 9:7).

But the experience of the Transfiguration was an experience of light also for Jesus . It was Abba's light projected on him, for him. It was like the experience of baptism renewed; Jesus was confirmed, once again, in his experience as the Father's beloved Son.

As he was about to take the road which led to Jerusalem, the Father confirmed him in the certainty that He was with him and that He would accompany him all the way until He could tell him, on Easter morning: 'You are my son, today I father you again' (Acts 13:33). As Jesus will say in the Upper Room, 'I am not alone, because the Father is with me' (John 16:32).

The Fruit of the Transfiguration

'After the voice had spoken, Jesus was found alone' (Luke 9:36). The conclusion of the story contrasts with the story itself; it is like an anticlimax.

Jesus alone: the daily Jesus, the Jesus of the Loaves, the Jesus of Caesarea. The disciples wanted to stay on the mountain, 'in the cloud.' But the Transfiguration is meant to be light on reality, not reality changed into something else. Actually, soon now, Jesus will take the road leading to Jerusalem. Luke puts it, 'As the time drew near for him to be taken up to heaven, he resolutely took the road to Jerusalem' (9:51), literally, he hardened his face towards Jerusalem.

Does that mean that the Transfiguration has not changed anything? It has not changed reality: Jesus is going to Jerusalem, and that will mean, not the triumphant, powerful, and rich Messianism the disciples dreamt of, but suffering and death. Jesus will be faithful, to the letter, to the programme announced in Caesarea.

But the grace of the Transfiguration is a new vision of that reality. To Jesus (and to the disciples?), the reality of the road to Jerusalem now appears not just as a road leading to suffering and failure, and death; it will also be the road on which the Beloved Son, accompanied by the Father, will walk towards the fulness of life. The Father's presence, both pillar of cloud and pillar of fire.

The Transfiguration in our own lives today

The Transfiguration story is, for us, an invitation to contemplate Jesus drenched in the Father's light; the 'daily Jesus', but also the Jesus of the Passion, already touched by the glory of Easter.

An invitation also to listen to Jesus, whatever his teaching, to take it, to accept it, to welcome it, as the teaching of the Beloved Son, even when he speaks of the cross, of conversion, of suffering. Jesus is 'the Way', always. Whoever follows him, listens to him, 'will not be walking in the dark, but will have the light of life' (John 8:12).

But the Transfiguration experience is not simply an experience enjoyed by Jesus and his three disciples on the high mountain in Galilee. It is also a grace offered to us as we journey on as disciples of Jesus. The grace of a new vision of reality.

Reality, the stuff of our daily lives, is not always easy to cope with. It has, of course, its hours of delight, moments which we would like to see last for ever: 'It is wonderful for us to be here' (Mark 9:5). But life has also its hours of darkness: hours marked by sorrow, by failure, by pain or sickness.

How do we try to cope with the harshness of reality in our daily lives? With a particularly difficult situation in our community, in our family? Or with the problems of ageing? Is it not true that we find it difficult, very difficult at times, simply to see, let alone to accept, reality as it is. We can spend so much energy trying to deny reality, or to bend it, manipulate it so as to make it suit our dreams. There are, of course, painful situations which we must do all we can to change. But so often, whether we like it or not, reality will stubbornly remain what it is, perhaps unpalatable, or even unacceptable, but here with us to stay.

Two experiences come to my mind at this point: the first is from Paul. Writing to the Christians of Corinth, Paul tells them about a problem in his own life: he calls it 'a thorn in the flesh'; we do not know what it was exactly; but one thing is certain, it irritated Paul, and again and again he prayed that the Lord might free him from his handicap. Paul's surprise was great when he heard the Lord tell him: 'My grace is sufficient for you, for power is made perfect in weakness' (II Corinthians 12:9). And through the Lord's grace, Paul was made able 'to see' the 'thorn in the flesh' which tormented him in another light; he could now see it as a unique chance for the Lord's love to display its power in an area where Paul felt so weak, so lost. And Paul could conclude: 'So, I will boast all the more gladly of my weaknesses, so that the power of Christ may dwell in me' (*ibid*)

The second experience is that of a Frenchman, Jacques Lebreton, who during World War II was very severely wounded in the battle for Tobrouk in Libya: a grenade burst in his hands, and he lost both hands and both eyes. He was immediately transported to the French hospital in Beyrouth; and there, he spent several days suffering atrociously. No one dared to tell him what had really happened to him; and he became more and more restless, demanding that the bandage that covered his eyes be taken off, so that he could get up and walk around. A French nurse finally decided to tell him the whole truth: 'Jacques, you have been very gravely wounded, you will never be able to see again, and you have lost both hands.' Jacques' reaction was that of a violent revolt which his Christian faith could not pacify: a revolt against war, against the hospital personnel, against life. The nurse who had told him about the reality of his condition did all she could to accompany him, to speak to him, to support him. The war over, Jacques was brought back to France. His revolt had not abated. He joined the communist party in order to give some form of political dimension to his anger. His nurse at the Beyrouth hospital had also gone back to France and he married her. And she did all she could to help Jacques to face, little by little, the harsh reality of his life as a severely handicapped young man. And Jacques did begin to journey, slowly, but surely, towards a new vision of his life, a new vision enlightened by his faith; he began to see that, even handicapped as he was, he could still live a worthwhile life. And the day came when he was able to write to the President of the Association for the Blind in France, asking him for an appointment. When he entered the President's office, the President immediately stood up and went to meet Jacques, offering to help him: 'What could I do for you?', he asked. And Jacques answered: 'Actually, I have come not to ask for help, but rather to offer my help.' To which the President said: 'But how could you help the Association since you have no eyes and no hands.' And Jacques replied: 'This is my great advantage over you: I know what it is to be blind, and I think I could help blind people, throughout France, to cope with their handicap.' Jacques' offer was accepted, and from then on, Jacques was able to travel all over France, giving conferences in order to sensitize people to the fate of the blind; helped by his wife, he wrote books about his 'journey' from Libya to Paris, from crippling handicaps to the great experience of living fully for others, and especially, for his blind brothers and sisters. As Jacques himself said many times, he was able to live to the full. He was still blind and had no hands, but he had been given the grace of discovering how much his handicap allowed him to live a life of loving service. Truly a grace of 'transfiguration', the grace of a renewed vision.

'This is my Son, the Beloved, listen to him'! The grace is offered to us all to discover, in the Father's light, brought to us by Jesus, the possibilities for love and service, perhaps often hidden, yet present, in every situation. And therefore, the possibilities every situation gives us to love, to live more abundantly, to live better; to help others live better.

But we must listen, listen attentively to Jesus: he is the Way to 'transfiguration', to a renewed vision. St John of the Cross expresses it aptly attributing these words to the Father: 'If I have already said all things to you in my Word, my Son, and if I have no other, what kind of answer could I give you now, or what could I reveal that would surpass this? Set your eyes on him alone, because in him I have said it all to you... and you will find in him even more than you are asking, more even than you desire... He is my total locution and vision, my total revelation and the whole of my reply. This I have already spoken to you... giving him to you as Brother, Companion, Master, Ransom and Reward' (*Ascent of Mount Carmel*, Book II).

9

Zacchaeus

It is so easy to please God
(*Luke 19:1-10*)

The disciples' journey was, from Caesarea to Jerusalem, a 'Passion-Journey', like Jesus' journey. It was, in some way, already, 'a way of the Cross.' Luke invites us to reflect at length on the demands made by Jesus on the people he had called to follow him (9:51-19:27). And there is, towards the end of Luke's story of the Journey to Jerusalem, a story which I find particularly important for the understanding of the journey of discipleship: it is the story of the encounter between Jesus and Zacchaeus.

The story of Zacchaeus was, until these past few years, a story with which I was very familiar but which did not really strike me. And then, one day, a reflection made to me by a Sister, a friend of mine, acted like a key which opened for me unsuspected riches in the Zacchaeus story. Sister Maureen was telling me about a directed retreat she had made a few years ago, and during which her director had invited her, one day, to spend that day in the company of Mary, Jesus' mother. And some time during that day, as Maureen was chatting with Mary about Jesus, Mary said to her these very simple words: 'You know, Maureen, it is so easy to please him'! These words stayed with me, and a few days later, they struck me as giving me the key to the understanding of the Zacchaeus story.

The Context of the Zacchaeus story in Luke's gospel

The Zacchaeus story is found only in Luke's gospel. Now, Luke's is the gospel of God's immense kindness and mercy: that is the fundamental message of Jesus in the third gospel; and this message reaches its climax during the Passion which, for Luke, is the epiphany of God's kindness and mercy.

God's kindness and mercy are given human form in and through Jesus: Jesus and the widow of Nain: 'Do not weep..., and he gave him to his mother' (Luke 7:13,15); Jesus and the woman who was a sinner: 'Your sins are forgiven, your faith has saved you, go in peace' (8:48,50); Jesus and the good thief on Calvary: 'Today you will be with me in Paradise' (23:43); Jesus and the people who crucified him: 'Father, forgive them, they do not know what they are doing' (23:34); and above all, at the very heart of Luke's gospel, the parable of the return of the Prodigal Son: 'This man welcomes sinners and eats with them' (15:2)—a parable in which Jesus unveils for us the Father's kind and merciful face. We could say that the story of Zacchaeus is in some way this parable becoming, through Jesus, an experience of life, in life.

A Story which is part of the long account of Jesus' Journey to Jerusalem. (9:51-19:27)

Jesus' journey towards Jerusalem and the Passion was about to come to an end: Luke's story had begun in 9:51 'When the days drew near for him to be taken up, Jesus set his face to go to Jerusalem'. It is a story which shows what must be the journey of the disciples called to follow Jesus.

And one of the major demands made on the disciples concerns riches. Perhaps should we note that the word 'riches' here stands for whatever we 'possess': money, things, but also talents, health, time, etc... Disciples should not possess riches, they should not cling to riches. Jesus' teaching on riches is well summed up in the conclusion of the story of the rich young man who had come to Jesus and enquired about what he should do to have eternal life: 'Jesus said to him, "There is still one thing lacking. Sell all that you own and distribute the money to the poor, and you will have treasure in heaven; then come, follow me." But when he heard this, he became sad; for he was very rich' (18:22-23)

And as the young man was going away, 'Jesus looked at him and said, "How hard it is for those who have wealth to enter the kingdom of God! Indeed, it is easier for a camel to go through the eye of a needle than for someone who is rich to enter the kingdom of God' (18:24-25).

These words of Jesus sound extremely radical, and with the disciples, we are entitled to ask: 'In that case, who can be saved?' (18:26).

Why does Jesus show himself so demanding when it comes to riches? Perhaps we could say that it was the experience of his ministry which led him to take such a radical stand. He often met people who found it difficult to accept him and his message: 'the learned and the clever' who 'knew', who thought they knew; people who 'possessed' learning, money, authority, influence, possessions of all sorts, and who so easily used them for themselves; their hands were full to capacity, and so were their hearts.

But Jesus also often met people who possessed little or nothing; they were the little ones, the poor; they welcomed Jesus, they spontaneously felt that the Good News preached by Jesus was for them. Having little, they were used to open their hands, and their hearts to welcome, to receive whatever was offered to them. For them, relying on the God of kindness and mercy was not a luxury, but a vital necessity; they filled Jesus with joy: 'At that same hour Jesus rejoiced in the Holy Spirit and said, "I thank you, Father, Lord of heaven and earth, because you have hidden these things from the wise and the intelligent and have revealed them to infants; yes, Father, for such was your gracious will. All things have been handed over to me by my Father; and no one knows who the Son is except the Father, or who the Father is except the Son and anyone to whom the Son chooses to reveal him"' (Luke 10:21-22).

To conclude Jesus' teaching on the danger of riches, let us quote again these very strong words: 'How hard it is for those who have riches to make their way into the Kingdom of God' (18:24).

Zacchaeus

Within this context, the story of Zacchaeus brings a breath of fresh air, and much hope (Luke 19:1-10). It is surely a story meant to give heart to those who are afraid; to give hope and trust to us all. There is so much good humour in the story, an ideal story to lead us into the encounter with Jesus that the retreat is meant to be.

'He entered Jericho and was passing through it. A man was there named Zacchaeus; he was a chief tax collector and was rich. He was trying to see who Jesus was, but on account of the crowd he could not, because he was short in stature. So he ran ahead and climbed a sycamore tree to see him, because he was going to pass that way. When Jesus came to the place, he looked up and said to him, "Zacchaeus, hurry and come down; for I must stay at your house today." So he hurried down and was happy to welcome him. All who saw it began to grumble and said, "He has gone to be the guest of one who is a sinner." Zacchaeus stood there and said to the Lord, "Look, half of my possessions, Lord, I will give to the poor; and if I have defrauded anyone of anything, I will pay back four times as much." Then Jesus said to him, "Today salvation has come to this house, because he too is a son of Abraham. For the Son of Man came to seek out and to save the lost."' (Luke 19:1-10).

Jericho

The town of Jericho is situated a few miles form Jerusalem. Jesus and his disciples have nearly reached the end of their long journey to the Holy City. Jesus, for the third time tells his disciples about his approaching Passion, but they simply 'do not understand what he is telling them' (Luke 18:34).

'He entered Jericho and was passing through it. A man was there named Zacchaeus; he was a chief tax collector and was rich' (Luke 19:1-2)

It takes only a few words for Luke to present Zacchaeus. He was a tax- collector, that is, in the Jewish society of Jesus' time, under Roman occupation, an enemy, on the side of the Romans who used tax-collectors to levy taxes on the Jews. He was an enemy, and a sinner, in constant contact with pagans and therefore permanently 'unclean.' Zacchaeus was, therefore, a marginal, someone whom Jewish society pushed into the margin and kept there, someone to be avoided by good, honest people.

But there was more: Zacchaeus was also 'a wealthy man'; and judging from Jesus' teaching on riches, that was his major handicap: 'Jesus looked at him [the rich young man] and said,

"How hard it is for those who have wealth to enter the kingdom of God! Indeed, it is easier for a camel to go through the eye of a needle than for someone who is rich to enter the kingdom of God.'" (Luke 18:24-25).

Luke, however has not yet told us everything about Zacchaeus. 'Zacchaeus was trying to see who Jesus was' (19:3). He was trying: he was not fully satisfied with his riches, there were still in him, in his heart, open, empty spaces.

He wanted *to see* Jesus, 'to catch a glimpse of Jesus' (as the Jerusalem Bible has it): he had heard about the prophet of Nazareth, the prophet who had just healed the blind man of Jericho (18:35-43, just before our story). Zacchaeus could not reasonably hope for more than a glimpse of Jesus; after all, he was a tax-collector.

He had, however, another handicap: he was quite small, and there were so many people accompanying Jesus, or standing on the roadside to see him that Zacchaeus could only hope to 'hear' Jesus passing by. But he found an original solution to his problem: 'He ran ahead and climbed a sycamore tree to see Jesus, because he was going to pass that way' (19:4). That, of course, would not take Zacchaeus very far in his knowledge of Jesus; but it might give some satisfaction to his curiosity.

Jesus sees...

'When Jesus came to the place, he looked up' (19:5). Jesus, Emmanuel, God among us, God revealed, God with a human face. Jesus must have felt, so to speak, the silent call of Zacchaeus' eyes; he stopped, and he looked at him. Zacchaeus may have felt a little ill-at-ease on his tree, but he could look at Jesus, and fill his eyes, and mind and heart with Jesus, his face, his eyes, his smile.

As the two men looked at each other, we can easily imagine the people of Jericho who surrounded Jesus, telling him, 'Don't waist your time with that fellow, he is a thief!'

Jesus speaks...

But it was not Jesus' way to dismiss people: 'this man welcomes sinners and eats with them...' (Luke 15:2). And Jesus spoke:

'Zacchaeus, hurry and come down; for I must stay at your house today.' (19:5).

Zacchaeus only wanted *to see*, nothing more. And now, Jesus was *speaking* to him: 'Zacchaeus...' Zacchaeus, the tax collector, the wealthy man, singled out. In a way, he was probably used to that; people always singled him out to laugh at him, to insult him, 'Zacchaeus, the tax-collector.

But now, it was different, totally different: Jesus was calling him by name, 'Zacchaeus'! And there was respect, friendship in Jesus' voice: 'I have called you by your name, your are mine, for you are precious in my eyes, and I love you' (Isaiah 43:1,4). Zacchaeus felt recognised, respected: he 'existed' for Jesus.

'Come down, hurry'. Jesus' call to Zacchaeus was not a word said 'by the way', without much attention. On the contrary, it expressed Jesus' desire for an encounter with Zacchaeus, a true, real encounter; an encounter which would be a great opportunity, a chance, not only for Zacchaeus, but also for Jesus. Jesus truly wanted, wished to encounter Zacchaeus; he had been wanting that encounter for so long. For an eternity! 'Zacchaeus, come down quickly.'

'I must stay at your house today' (19:5). 'I *must*', the obligation, the 'must' of friendship, of love. In Luke's gospel, the verb used here by the Evangelist refers to Jesus' mission, culminating in his Passover (Luke 2:49; 12:50; 24:26). 'I must: that is why I have come.'

'I must *stay* at your house' (19:5): the verb 'to stay' implies time. Jesus does not have in mind a short, flying visit. He wants to 'stay', to abide: 'He has gone to stay at a sinner's house' (19:7). 'To stay', however, does not translate exactly the verb used by Luke which means, literally, 'to unwind, to unharness, 'to relax'. 'I must unharness, relax'; and Jesus does not see any better way to relax than to stay at Zacchaeus' house. Zacchaeus, of all people!

The way the story is told, we are under the impression that it was Jesus who asked Zacchaeus for a favour.

The Encounter

'Zacchaeus hurried down and welcomed Jesus joyfully' (19:6). We imagine Zacchaeus tumbling down from the tree, hardly believing the words he had just heard: 'He, Jesus, the prophet of Nazareth, has spoken to me, and he is coming to my house!' The welcome he gave to Jesus necessarily included a meal; a meal which expressed mutual respect and acceptance, friendship and communion: 'This man welcomes sinners and eats with them.'

There is a tremendous contrast between what Zacchaeus sought when he was alone on his sycamore tree—just to see Jesus lost in the crowd—and what Jesus gave him: a face to face encounter. God's way revealed in and through Jesus; God, in Jesus, seeking to meet us face to face, far beyond anything we could have asked or imagined: 'Jesus, the prophet from Nazareth in my house, here, sitting, and talking to me.'

But 'they all complained: He has gone to stay at a sinner's house'; 'this man welcomes sinners and eats with them'—the scandal of God's immense love and mercy revealed in and through Jesus. It must have been one of Jesus' greatest joys.

Love's Response to Love

Zacchaeus was now more, much more than the senior tax-collector of Jericho; he knew he was someone Jesus loved, someone who had given hospitality to Jesus. The rest was bound to follow, but it only followed: 'Zacchaeus stood there and said to the Lord, "Look, half of my possessions, Lord, I will give to the poor; and if I have defrauded anyone of anything, I will pay back four times as much' (19:8).

A resolution, a promise which was the response of Zacchaeus' love to Jesus'; it had the quality, the strength of this love. His encounter with Jesus had made him 'a true son of Abraham', a 'believer', someone who had put his faith in God, in Jesus; it was God, revealed in Jesus, and not power or money, who was now the rock on which his life would rest.

How easy it is to please God!

One of the conclusions which I draw from Zacchaeus' experience is how 'easy it really is to please God', to please Jesus.

Judging from Jesus' words on riches, Zacchaeus' chances of ever entering the kingdom were practically nil: 'How hard it is for those who have riches to make their way into the Kingdom of God' (18:24); or, again, 'None of you can be my disciple without giving up all that he owns' (14:33).

Taken out of their context, these words could frighten, discourage us! And in order to escape from God's demands, we could make of our life an endless search for perfection; always trying to do more, to suffer more, to pray more, as if, we could make it through our own efforts.

Zacchaeus' story opens for us a totally different perspective: it was Jesus' mission to reveal to the world the immensely kind and compassionate face of God. That is the necessary context within which we must read, and understand the gospels. In Luke's gospel, we are given, in the story of the father of 'the Prodigal Son', a glimpse of how far God's mercy is prepared to go—a God who loves us infinitely and begs us to love him with all our heart, with all our soul, and with all our strength (see Luke 10:27). But at the same time, precisely because He loves us, a God whom the slightest loving gesture on our part, or the smallest desire coming out of our heart, moves to compassion: 'Hurry, come down, I must stay with you today' (19:5).

We must read the Zacchaeus story in the present tense: it is our story. We must, like Zacchaeus, let Jesus' eyes meet ours; we must let him speak to us, and come and abide with us. The rest—far beyond anything we could imagine or ask for—can follow. But are we willing to climb up a sycamore tree, like Zacchaeus, in order to have a glimpse of Jesus?

10

'That they may all be one...'
The hour has come
(John 17)

'Come, follow me...' Having followed Jesus step by step, the disciples are now gathered around him in Jerusalem, at the time of the Passover: 'The hour has come', as John puts it. The hour towards which Jesus' life and ministry were directed (John 2:4); the hour of Jesus' supreme revelation of the Father, the hour of Jesus' passion, death and resurrection, the hour of love's supreme gift: 'Now before the festival of the Passover, Jesus knew that his hour had come to depart from this world and go to the Father. Having loved his own who were in the world, he loved them to the end.' (John 13:1-2).

Jesus' hour began with a meal celebrated within the context of the Passover. Table-companionship was, as we know, very important to Jesus as a sacrament of the Father's immense and merciful kindness. Therefore, we are not surprised that Jesus chose to spend the last few hours of freedom that were left to him, sharing a meal with his disciples. More than ever, he wanted to let them experience how close he was to them. He wanted to make them feel, as always, accepted, respected, loved, whatever might happen.

We find the story of the Last Supper in the four gospels. But whereas, in the gospels of Mark, Matthew and Luke, the story takes a fairly limited number of verses, John devotes five chapters to it. In these chapters, 13 to 17, Jesus' last words to his disciples are focused mainly on relationships—the relationship which ought to bind them to Jesus, and through him to the Father, and the relationship which must bind them to one another.

Jesus concludes his message to his disciples with a lengthy prayer for them: 'After Jesus had spoken these words, he looked up to heaven and said, "Father, the hour has come; glorify your Son so that the Son may glorify you, since you have given him authority over all people, to give eternal life to all whom you have given him.'" (John 17:1-3).

Father, the hour has come, glorify your Son (John 17:1)

Jesus' prayer is directed to the Father. The Father's name appears six times in this text: Jesus is turned full faced towards the Father, towards the Source—the Father-Abba, the God who is so near, so intimate, so full of kindness and mercy. As Jesus is about to leave his disciples to enter into his passion, he expresses what inhabits his own heart, and Abba's heart—a heart to heart prayer. And we listen in, because we are invited to.

Jesus prays for his disciples 'I am asking on their behalf; on behalf of those whom you gave me, because they are yours.' (17:9).

The disciples were obviously always present to Jesus' mind and heart. And now they are truly at the forefront of his concern. Out of 26 verses in John chapter 17, twentythree are connected, in some way or other, with the disciples. The disciples are truly at the centre of Jesus' prayer, at the centre of Jesus' preoccupations.

How does Jesus see them? What are they to him? How does he speak about them to the Father? One of the keywords in chapter 17 is, beyond any doubt, the verb 'to give'; it occurs fifteen times in that chapter. Everything is gift, everything is a gift from the Father: the power displayed by Jesus during his ministry (17:2); the work he has accomplished (17:4); the words he has spoken (17:8); the Father's name he has revealed to his disciples (17:6,26), everything, 'All I have is yours and all you have is mine.'

But the greatest gift of all Jesus received from the Father, was and is *his disciples*: 'those you have given me '(the expression recurs seven times in chapter 17): that he may give eternal life to those you have given him (v 2); 'I have revealed your name to those you took from the world to give me; they were yours and you gave them to me' (v 6); 'I am not praying for the world, but for those you have given me' (v 9).

The disciples, all disciples, are the Father's gift to Jesus; they belong to Jesus, they belong to the Father; they are the Father's and Jesus' concern. We must listen at length to such words; we must listen on and on, until we finally begin to hear what these words say—what they say about us, about me. They have the power to change radically the vision we have of God, of ourselves, of people, of members of our community. They will lead us to adore in awe the love with which God embraces all of us; they will fill our hearts with gratitude, with boundless trust, and deep joy.

Holy Father, protect them from the world...' (John 17:11)

In his final prayer, Jesus seems to voice three major preoccupations concerning his disciples: the way they must relate to the world, the relationship which should bind them to one another, and finally, Jesus' will to see them gathered around him for ever in the Father's home.

The Relationship between the Disciples and the World

'Now I am no longer in the world, but they are in the world, and I am coming to you. Holy Father, protect them in your name that you have given me, so that they may be one, as we are one...' (John 17:11-12, 14-19).

The keywords are easy to trace in these verses: 'the world' appears 8 times in 9 verses; and it is accompanied with words such as 'keep, watch, protect.' We are thus given the impression that, for Jesus, the relationship of disciples to the world is a necessary, but difficult one, full of dangers for the disciples who, therefore, must be protected.

The World as the place for Mission for the Disciples

In John's gospel in particular, the word 'world' points to an ambiguous reality. It points first of all to 'the place of mission for the disciples': the disciples are in the world, like Jesus, the world which God loves so much that he gave his only Son to save (John 3:16).

Jesus, unlike John the Baptist, unlike the Qumran monks was not a man of the desert, but a man of towns and villages (Matthew 9:35); he did not wait for people to come and see him, he went to them; and he wanted his disciples to be like him, 'I am not asking you to remove them from the world' (17:15).

Thus in the world, the disciples must continue Jesus' mission: 'As you have sent me into the world, I have sent them into the world' (17:18). Like Jesus, therefore, they must live in solidarity with the world, especially with the little ones, the poor, the marginalised, those who are most in need of love. They must know, love, live with them, share with them, so that they may come to know that God is a God of love and compassion, that God is Abba, and find in God, life and life to the full' (John 10:10).

The World as a Value-System opposed to the Gospel

The same word, 'world', also refers, in John's gospel, to a value-system opposed to the gospel; and therefore, to a reality which is dangerous for the disciples: 'They belong to the world no more than I belong to the world' (17:14).

How does Jesus, in John's gospel, characterise the world which 'hates the disciples', precisely because they are disciples of Jesus (17:14)? He sees the world as lying in the power of 'the evil one': 'Protect them from the evil one' (17:15). And 'the evil one', in John's gospel, is above all the great liar: 'I am not asking you to take them out of the world, but I ask you to protect them from the evil one. They do not belong to the world, just as I do not belong to the world. Sanctify them in the truth; your word is truth' (17:15-17).

These words echo a much stronger statement which John puts on Jesus' lips in a discussion with the Jewish leaders in Jerusalem: 'You are from your father the devil, and you choose to do your father's desires. He was a murderer from the beginning and does not stand in the truth, because there is no truth in him. When he lies, he speaks according to his own nature, for he is a liar and the father of lies. But because I tell the truth, you do not believe me.' (John 8:44-45).

What then is Jesus' Message for us today?

Jesus does not want us to run away. Our mission-field, as disciples of Jesus, is the world—a world in which we must not be afraid. We are in the Father's hand. But at the same time, we must not be naive, we must be realistic. We can easily be contaminated by the value-system which the world holds, a value-system in which truth is often, at best, marginalised.

I find the Temptation Story in the gospels of Matthew and Luke very helpful to understand how far we can become used to living by half-truths, or even at times, blatant lies. In the Temptation Story, the Devil offers to Jesus a vision of life permeated with falsehood: the falsehood of 'self-service' as a basic principle of living ('tell these stones to turn into loaves', that is, use the gifts and powers you have been given to look after yourself); the falsehood of self-glorification, of immediate personal success ('If you are the Son of God, throw yourself down', God will necessarily protect you and people will immediately acclaim you as the Messiah); the falsehood of power and riches ('I will give you all these if you fall at my feet and do me homage'). Whatever the stage at which we are on our journey as disciples of Jesus, we find it difficult to be, like Jesus, 'servants' of God's kindness and mercy. And the world in which we live constantly invites us to think first of ourselves, to worship ourselves.

This raises the question of the demands made on us by what I call 'gospel-ecology.' We tend to be so 'green', so naive; we live, at times, as if we did not need a 'gospel environment', a gospel environment which we must make for ourselves, for our communities, so as to be able to live out the gospel values. We must live in, and with, the world today, in solidarity with the world. But as disciples of Jesus, whose lives are truly inspired by the gospel values. We must be true about it all, and honest, with God's Word as our guide. Jesus shows us the way.

'That they may be one'

Jesus' second major concern as he is about to leave his disciples to enter into his Passion, is that of the bond which must keep them at one with one another; he speaks twice about it in his prayer to the Father, in John 17:11 and 17:20-23

'And now I am no longer in the world, but they are in the world, and I am coming to you. Holy Father, protect them in your name that you have given me, so that they may be one, as we are one...'

Behind this insistence of Jesus, there was obviously the situation of the Christian communities, especially in Asia Minor, at the end of the first century a.d. Christian communities were spread far and wide, but they had to face, in many places, persecutions coming especially from Roman officials who sought to impose the cult of the emperor throughout the empire. Persecutions did keep Christians on their toes, but they also were a severe test for their faith. Behind the anger and violence found in the Book of Revelation, there was the question which must have haunted the minds of so many Christians: 'Where is the Risen Lord? Why does not the Risen Lord, the conqueror of sin and death, affirm his victory now over the enemies of our faith?' Persecutions could bring Christians closer to one another; they could also frighten them into giving up their faith. It was essential that Christian communities be firmly held together by a deep bond of faith and love.

The end of the first century saw also the emergence of the first heresies. The Johannine writings' insistence on the full reality of the Incarnation suggests that the danger of Christian communities being torn apart by heresy, was not just a possibility (see I John 2:18-23).

The Church's situation today may be different from that of the early Church. Jesus' call to unity is nevertheless just as essential today as it was then. And it is directed not just to the Church at large, or to the Church's leaders, but to each one of us. We are all called to be, as disciples of Jesus, unity-makers, bridge-builders.

The unity Jesus has in mind in chapter 17 is not just any type of unity. It must be modelled on the unity that binds together Father and Son; it must be communion of life, communion of love, '...one, just as you, Father, are in me and I am in you' (17:21)—the unity, the at-oneness, the living at-oneness of Father and Son, the at-oneness of divine 'pre-existence', so beautifully expressed in Roublev's icon of the Trinity.

It was this unity that Jesus sought to achieve through his ministry. He not only preached the Good News of the Kingdom of God, he made it begin to happen. He offered welcome, respect, forgiveness, healing to all, especially to the poor, to the marginalised, all of them beloved daughters and sons of Abba.

The unity Jesus prays for for his disciples is not a unity, an at-oneness which they could attain just by themselves; it is a gift, a grace to be prayed for. At the same time, it must be a programme demanding from us true commitment.

How then do Jesus' words challenge us, how do they challenge me? Am I, are we as a community, interested, involved in any way in inter-church relations, or do I, do we think that that is a problem for Church authorities and theologians? Jesus saw unity between his disciples as the first and greatest gospel witness they could give to the world: 'May all be one. As you, Father, are in me and I am in you, may they also be in us, so that the world may believe that you have sent me. The glory that you have given me I have given them, so that they may be one, as we are one, I in them and you in me, that they may become completely one, so that the world may know that you have sent me and have loved them even as you have loved me' (John 17:21-23).

Surely, Jesus' words should prompt us not only to pray for the unity of all Christians, but also to seek to know what is going on in ecumenism, to know how Christians belonging to Churches other than ours understand the gospel and express their faith.

Working for the unity of all Christians must not be just a hobby; it is our duty as Jesus' disciples. Unity-seeking must be in us, an attitude of mind, a mentality, a vision. It must be the expression of a faith-inspired desire to be like Jesus in all our relationships, beginning with our relationships within our imme-diate community: unity-makers, bridge-builders. How could we be interested in inter-church unity if, in our daily lives, we refuse to accept people who are different from us, or if we show ourselves to be intolerant?

Taking seriously Jesus' call for unity will bring us to a basic attitude of loving acceptance, respect, non-aggression. We will shun away from uniformity which so easily steamrolls people, ideas, relationships. Instead, we will seek to accept, and welcome diversity, knowing how to discern between what really matters, and what does not, remembering Paul VI's golden words: 'Only the Kingdom is absolute, and it makes everything else relative' (*Evangelisation in the Modern World*, 8).

Writing about Jesus' mission of unity, the author of the Letter to the Ephesians writes: 'He is the peace between us, and has made the two into one entity and broken down the barrier which used to keep them apart, by destroying in his own person the hostility' (Ephesians 2:14, JB).

We cannot continue Jesus' mission unless, like him, we too refuse to let the hostility which is rooted in our hearts inspire our attitude to people. In sacramental terms, it means to be willing, like Jesus, to be 'bread broken and shared' for others.

'I want them to be with me where I am' (John 17: 24-26)

'Father, I desire that those also, whom you have given me, may be with me where I am, to see my glory, which you have given me because you loved me before the foundation of the world. Righteous Father, the world does not know you, but I know you; and these know that you have sent me. I made your name known to them, and I will make it known, so that the love with which you have loved me may be in them, and I in them' (John 17:24-26)

We have now reached the conclusion of Jesus' prayer, a conclusion in which Jesus expresses a desire which must have been foremost in his mind and heart: 'I desire that my disciples to be with me where I am' (17:24). It was actually with similar words that Jesus had opened his Last Supper Discourse: 'In my Father's house there are many dwelling places. If it were not so, would I have told you that I go to prepare a place for you? And if I go and prepare a place for you, I will come again and will take you to myself, so that where I am, there you may be also' (14:2-3).

These are words which we must especially cherish. They are about us, and they should fill our hearts with joyful hope. They are addressed to the Father, the God whom Jesus has invited us to call 'Abba-Father'. Now, when Jesus prays to the Father, his favourite words seem to be, 'Father, your will be done' (see Mark 14:36); the very words he has taught us: 'You should pray like this: Father, your will be done' (Matthew 6:9-10). Here, however, as Jesus is about to leave the Upper Room and go to the garden of Gethsemane, other words come to his lips: 'Father, I desire that those you have given me, may be with me where I am' (17:24).

'I desire': the verb used here may not have the compulsive

strength of 'I want', yet it does express a desire which seems to be particularly important to Jesus. His disciples are, we are, his 'friends' (John 15:13-15), they are close to him, he wants them to be with him for ever; and he knows his Father's thinking on the matter: 'The Father and I are one' (10:30).

Truly, we can say with Paul: 'If God is for us, who is against us? ... Who will separate us from the love of Christ? ... I am convinced that neither death, nor life, nor angels, nor rulers, nor things present, nor things to come, nor powers, nor height, nor depth, nor anything else in all creation, will be able to separate us from the love of God in Christ Jesus our Lord' (Romans 8:31,35,38-39).

Truly, our hope and our joy are rooted, not in our own achievements, but in the love with which Jesus embraces us all. In Gethsemane, Mark tell us, when Jesus was arrested, all his disciples 'deserted him and ran away' (Mark 14:50). Jesus never deserted them, and he will give them the supreme proof of his love and fidelity: 'No one has greater love than this, to lay down one's life for one's friends' (John 15:13).

11

Gethsemane
Companions of Jesus in his Agony
(Mark 14:32-42)

The Passion Narratives in the Gospels
'When they had sung the hymn, they went out to the Mount of Olives' (Mark 14:26)

As we enter Jesus' Passion, we once again remember his words to his disciples when he met them for the first time: 'Come, follow me, I will make you fish for people' (Mark 1:17). We listen attentively to these words of Jesus as, his last meal with his disciples being over, he goes down with them to the Kedron valley, and begins to climb the Mount of Olives: 'come, follow me.'

'Come, follow me', now especially because the hour has come, the crucial moment which will mark the climax of Jesus' life and ministry, of Jesus' journey.. An 'hour' of passion, filled to the brim with Jesus' love, 'love to the end' (John 13:1); an 'hour' of passion also, because it will be filled with intense suffering.

The passion of Jesus is given a prominent place in the four gospels. Seemingly, it lasted less than twenty four hours; and yet the evangelists give us detailed narratives covering several chapters. At first sight, the gospel narratives of the passion seem to give us precise accounts of 'what happened', from Gethsemane to Golgotha. But actually, if the evangelists' accounts agree on essentials concerning the unfolding of Jesus' passion, the main aim of these accounts is to offer us a catechesis based on the major moments of the passion. In other words, the evangelists do not want us to be present to Jesus' passion simply as spectators; they want us to join the disciples, and the women accompanying Jesus, so as to let Jesus' forgiving love stir our hearts into gratitude and an intense desire to continue with Jesus our journey as disciples.

And thus, we have, in the gospels, four different catecheses, four different approaches to the mystery of Jesus' passion and death. Mark (chapters 14-15) and Matthew (chapters 26-27) seem to put a particular stress on Jesus' loneliness, though Matthew does show the whole universe siding with Jesus crucified. Luke (chapters 22-23), on the contrary, sees Jesus' passion as the great 'epiphany' of God's mercy revealed in and through Jesus and drawing already together pagans and Jews. As to John (chapters 18-19), he presents Jesus' passion as the solemn liturgy of the birth of a new humankind: Jesus on the cross is the New Adam from whose side is born the new Eve, the Church.

It is important not to try to bring together these four stories of Jesus' passion 'in order to have a complete account of what happened.' We must, on the contrary, respectfully and grate-fully read and meditate each story for itself and let it bring us nearer to 'the breadth and length, the height and the depth of God's love revealed in Jesus on the Cross' (see Ephesians 3:18-19).

We are going to ask Mark to bring us to the Garden of Gethsemane and to help us 'to watch and pray' with Jesus in agony.

Gethsemane

'They went to a place called Gethsemane; and he said to his disciples, "Sit here while I pray."' (Mark 14:32-33).

To begin with, let us focus our attention on the actors of the drama which is about to unfold in the garden of Gethsemane. And first, Jesus of Nazareth.

Jesus, the prophet from Galilee, a prophet 'powerful in ac-tion and speech before God and the whole people' (Luke 24:19). He was the prophet who spent so much time with the poor, with the sick for whom he made the Good News of the Kingdom begin to become reality. We remember the scene so often de-scribed by the gospels: 'Jesus departed with his disciples to the sea, and a great multitude from Galilee followed him; hearing all that he was doing, they came to him in great numbers from Judaea, Jerusalem, Idumaea, beyond the Jordan, and the region around Tyre and Sidon. He told his disciples to have a boat ready for him because of the crowd, so that they would not crush him; for he had cured many, so that all who had diseases pressed upon him to touch him ' (Mark 3:7-10)

One thing is sure about Jesus, the Galilean prophet: 'He did save others', legions of them (see Mark 15:29-32).

Jesus, the prophet, was also, as were all prophets, a teacher whose message was always one of encouragement, of trust. Speaking to the disciples who were to go ahead of him to prepare the way for him, he said: 'Do not fear those who kill the body but cannot kill the soul; rather fear him who can destroy both soul and body in hell. Are not two sparrows sold for a penny? Yet not one of them will fall to the ground apart from your Father. And even the hairs of your head are all counted. So do not be afraid; you are of more value than many sparrows' (Matthew 10: 28-31).

Jesus' utter confidence and trust found their source in the God whom he called 'Abba', a name which, as we know, spelt nearness, kindness, compassion. And therefore, Jesus' constant invitation was, 'Do not be afraid.'

Peter, James and John...

'They went to a place called Gethsemane; and he said to his disciples, "Sit here while I pray." He took with him Peter and James and John' (Mark 14:32-33).

According to Mark and Matthew, when Jesus reached the garden of Gethsemane on the Mount of Olives, he left at the gate, so to speak, eight of his disciples, and with three of them, Peter, James and John, he went further into the garden.

Peter, James and John were among the first to have been called by Jesus on the shore of Lake Tiberias (Mark 1:16-20). And thus, they were Jesus' companions from the beginning of his ministry. They were also privileged witnesses of some major moments in Jesus' ministry: they were with Jesus when he raised Jairus' daughter back to life (Mark 5:35-43); they were his companions on the Mountain of Transfiguration (Mark 9:2-8). And now, Jesus was inviting them to be with him as he prayed. We may, therefore, suppose that they were closer to Jesus than other disciples, they must have known him better, they could, in some way, feel with him, and for him.

They were certainly also generous men, full of promises and hopes. During the Last Supper, as Jesus was trying to prepare them for the painful events which he could sense were imminent, Peter had told him, 'Even though I must die with you, I will not deny you." And Mark added: 'All of them said the same' (14:31).

But Peter, James and John were also great dreamers. In many ways, they shared the dreams of their contemporaries concerning the Messiah who was about to come: he would make his people free from the Roman yoke, and would 'restore the kingdom in favour of Israel' (see Acts 1:6); they hoped that the Prophet from Nazareth would be that Messiah, and therefore they, as Jesus' companions, would be given a share in his power and authority: 'James and John, the sons of Zebedee, came forward to him and said to him, "Teacher, we want you to do for us whatever we ask of you." And he said to them, "What is it you want me to do for you?" And they said to him, "Grant us to sit, one at your right hand and one at your left, in your glory"' (Mark 10:35-37).

Because of their messianic expectations, Peter, James and John were not prepared to face what was going to happen. They were so attached to their dreams that they found it impossible to believe that Jesus was serious when he spoke of the difficulties lying ahead. Their only hope will be Jesus' fidelity to his love for them.

'Jesus began to be distressed and agitated' (Mark 14:33)

As we read Mark's story of Jesus' agony, we are struck by the apparent suddenness of a change of mood in Jesus: in the Upper Room, it is true, the atmosphere was charged with tension: Jesus knew that Judas was about to betray him; he sensed that neither Peter, nor the other disciples would be able to face a situation in which Jesus himself would be defeated. But Jesus accepted that, and he already offered himself for his disciples, for the world, whatever might happen: 'My Body for you, my Blood for you'! Jesus was willing to die to fulfil his mission.

Yet, when he arrived at Gethsemane, a place where he used to retire for the night when he was in Jerusalem with his disciples (see Luke 22:39), all of a sudden, he was struck with panic, a totally new experience for him. Why? Perhaps we can understand a little if we take into account the geographical situation of the Mount of Olives. The Mount of Olives is situated east of Jerusalem from which it is separated by the Kedron valley. When Jesus reached it, and entered into the garden of Gethsemane, he realised that the time had come for him to take a final decision, his final decision: he could still escape. A man of his age (Jesus was then about thirty five years old) could easily take advantage of darkness to run, unnoticed, up to the top of the Mount of Olives, and from there, go down, through the Judaean desert, towards the Jordan river, cross the river, and perhaps continue his ministry there.

But, of course, Jesus could also decide to stay and wait for his enemies.

He therefore had to take a crucial decision, no longer in the relative security of the Upper Room, but in the threatening obscurity of Gethsemane.

As the Letter to the Hebrews puts it, Jesus was 'tempted in every way that we are, though he is without sin' (Hebrews 4:15). How, therefore, could he not be deeply distressed as he was about to take a decision which for him was a matter of life or death?

Jesus' Agony

When the evangelists set about writing the story of Jesus' agony at Gethsemane, they must have been filled with awe before the tremendous mystery of Jesus' distress. Each one approaches it in his own way. Luke does all he can to soften Jesus' pain; Jesus does not appear to be perturbed, or restless, and above all, he receives comfort directly from heaven, the comfort which gives him the strength to confront a most violent battle (Luke 22:39-46). John omits altogether the scene of the agony. As soon as Jesus reaches the garden of Gethsemane, his enemies arrive and arrest him (John 18:1-3).

What about Mark and Matthew? Mark, followed by Matthew, was struck by Jesus' loneliness, and Jesus' question to Peter, 'Simon, are you asleep? Could you not keep awake one hour?' (Mark 14:37) expresses powerfully how lonely Jesus felt. Mark will be our guide and will help us to accompany Jesus in his agony.

'Jesus took with him Peter and James and John, and began to be distressed and agitated. And said to them, "I am deeply grieved, even to death; remain here, and keep awake"' (Mark 14:33-34)

'Distressed, agitated, deeply grieved...': 'distressed', probably too mild a translation of a Greek word which Vincent Taylor, one of the leading commentators of Mark's gospel, translates 'shuddering with horror.' 'Agitated': that is, anguished, afraid of what is to come. 'Deeply grieved': even to death; sad to the point of death; an overwhelming sadness.

And these words and expressions are about Jesus whom we have so often heard say to this disciples: 'Do not be afraid, your Father knows...!'

But why was Jesus 'terrified'? He knew that his enemies wanted to arrest him, and he also knew that if he fell into their hands, they would show no pity: prophets, before him, had been tortured, and killed. There was also the prospect of death coming so soon to him. He was only about thirty-five years old, and he was too human not to love the precious life he had received from the Father. And above all, perhaps, there must have been, in Jesus' heart, a sense of failure: he would not be able to complete his mission. A look at the three disciples who had followed him into the garden of Gethsemane, was enough to show him how much more time, how much more work it would take him to give them all that they needed to continue his mission. And there was also his failure to open his people's minds to the riches of the Kingdom. We find, in the Last Supper discourses in John's gospel, words which express in a poignant fashion what Jesus felt as he saw his final hour approaching: 'If I had not come and spoken to them [my people], they would not have sin; but now they have no excuse for their sin... If I had not done among them the works that no one else did, they would not have sin.

But now they have seen and hated both me and my Father'. (John 15:22,24) In some way, Jesus felt that his very mission had brought about the negative reaction of his people.

We must take time to let all these words echo in our hearts. They call not just for our attention, but for our compassion. They invite us to dwell, to abide with Jesus, and to let him tell us about his own feelings and emotions as he is about to be arrested.

How did Jesus try to cope with the agonising battle that faced him? As always, Jesus sought light and strength in prayer, but a prayer which was itself a battle: 'And going a little farther, he threw himself on the ground and prayed that, if it were possible, the hour might pass from him. He said, "Abba, Father, for you all things are possible; remove this cup from me; yet, not what I want, but what you want"' (Mark 14:35-36).

'Abba!' It is the only time that the word 'Abba' appears in Mark's gospel. There is something deeply moving in this call to 'Abba - Daddy - God', springing out of Jesus' distress: 'He threw himself on the ground and prayed...Abba'!

The Mystery of Abba's and Jesus' battle against evil

But what I find more striking still, in a way, in Mark's story of Jesus' agony, is Jesus' restlessness. Jesus did want to find strength and comfort in Abba's presence. Yet, at the same time, because he was truly one of us 'in all things but sin' (Hebrews 4:15), he needed the presence, the support of his disciples, of those who were nearest to him. And Mark shows us Jesus going three times from prayer to his disciples: 'He came and found them sleeping; and he said to Peter, "Simon, are you asleep? Could you not keep awake one hour?"... And again he went away and prayed, saying the same words. And once more he came and found them sleeping,... He came a third time and said to them, "Are you still sleeping and taking your rest? Enough! The hour has come; the Son of Man is betrayed into the hands of sinners"' (Mark 14:37-41). 'We will never contemplate enough the abyss of the holy humanity of our God.'[1]

How disappointed Jesus must have been when he found that

his disciples were actually incapable of sharing in any way in his agony: Mark insists on this; he shows Jesus 'going on a little further', away from his three companions, in order to pray. Thus there was a 'physical distance' between Jesus at prayer and the three men; but that 'physical distance' was also a symbol of a much greater distance. Peter, James and John were, psychologically, spiritually, absent, foreign to Jesus' experience. Jesus had invited them to 'watch and pray', to be at one with him; instead, they 'slept': the word recurs three times. They were not just distant, they were away, in another world.

And why could they not be 'with Jesus', as they had been called to? Because they were not, since the episode of the loaves, on Jesus' wavelength; they could have followed, be with, a Jesus who would have been the Jesus of their dreams; the real Jesus was beyond them. In a moment, when Jesus' enemies came to arrest him, 'they would all desert him and run away' (Mark 14:50). It would be, seemingly, the end of their 'journey' as disciples.

As a result, Jesus in Gethsemane was terribly lonely, a loneliness which, in Mark's story, nothing came to soften. Could we say that Abba, at least, heard and answered Jesus' prayer? According to Luke, an angel came to comfort Jesus, 'An angel from heaven appeared to him and gave him strength.'

But the angel's presence seemed to increase the violence of Jesus' inner struggle: 'In his anguish he prayed more earnestly, and his sweat became like great drops of blood falling down on the ground' (Luke 22:43-44).

There is no angel in Mark's story, yet, we are made to understand that Jesus received from Abba the strength to face his enemies: 'He came a third time and said to them, "Are you still sleeping and taking your rest? Enough! The hour has come; the Son of Man is betrayed into the hands of sinners. Get up, let us be going. See, my betrayer is at hand"' (Mark 14:41-42)

Jesus' Agony and us today

The gospels' story of Jesus' agony is, first of all, an invitation to contemplate at length Jesus in his passion and, therefore, God revealed in Jesus' agony — God, in Jesus, revealed as immensely vulnerable, out of love.

Two quotations from the Letter to the Hebrews may help us in our contemplation: 'He had to become like his brothers and sisters in every respect, so that he might be a merciful and faithful high priest in the service of God, to make a sacrifice of atonement for the sins of the people. Because he himself was tested (tempted) by what he suffered, he is able to help those who are being tested. (Hebrews 2:17-18).

'We do not have a high priest who is unable to sympathize with our weaknesses, but we have one who in every respect has been tested (tempted) as we are, yet without sin' (Hebrews 4:15)

The 'understanding Christ', the 'understanding God' of Gethsemane

But the story of Jesus' agony is also an invitation 'to watch and pray today'. As Blaise Pascal puts it, 'Jesus is in agony until the end of the world, we must not sleep during that time.' We must therefore be willing to let Jesus tell us today: 'I am now in agony, can you come and visit me, and comfort me with your presence...'?

The story of Jesus' agony always reminds me of a story told by a French writer, Gilbert Cesbron, about a friend of his (let us call him John), who had been feeling very tired for some time. He finally decided to go and see a doctor. He underwent a number of tests, and a few days later, he had to go back to his doctor so as to know the results of the tests. But on that day, he and his wife were to receive a group of their friends and have a party with them. Just before he left home to go to the doctor, John said to his wife who was working in the kitchen, preparing the party: 'I am going to the doctor to get the result of the tests.' As she was very busy, she did not answer. John felt very apprehensive, and when his doctor told him that the tests had revealed that he had a large tumour, so large that an operation would be impossible, he felt as if he was going to die. The doctor did promise him that he would do all he could to help him, but that was little comfort for John. He went back home, and found his wife still busy in the kitchen. He said to her, 'Could I have a word with you'; but her reaction was sharp: 'our friends will be here shortly, and I still have a lot of work to do, we will talk later.'

John then went upstairs and knocked at the room of one of his daughters who was studying at university: 'could I have a word with you', he asked her. But she too was busy: 'Dad, I have a major exam tomorrow, excuse me.' And so John had to wait; he had to go through the ordeal of a long and noisy party. And finally, when the friends had all gone, he went again to the kitchen where his wife was busy clearing up things. She did not seem to be in a mood to listen or to talk; but this time, John put his hands firmly on her shoulders, and said to her: 'Mary, you must now listen to me', and he told her the news; she was terribly upset and felt ashamed.

Praying over Jesus' passion is difficult, austere; we must accept Jesus' invitation: 'watch and pray.' We must be there in solidarity with Jesus, out of compassion for him, wanting to be with him, for his own sake. Jesus must be at the centre of our prayer; we want to follow him, to contemplate him, listen to him.

And Jesus in Agony will, in some way or other, send us on a mission to people who are 'in agony now', perhaps in our own family, or community. We must be disciples that far, today.

12

Golgotha: Jesus dies on the Cross
'Come, follow me'
(Mark 1:17)

Once again, we must recall Jesus' words when he called his first disciples: 'Come, follow me, I will make you fishers of people'. But now, these words take on a new meaning. They come from Jesus at Calvary, from the dying Jesus; and they are like a cry in the desert, because the men Jesus had met and called on the shore of Lake Tiberias have 'deserted him and run away' (Mark 14:50); they can no longer hear their Master's words. Their journey as disciples has ended in shame. They have abandoned Jesus at the moment he needed them most.

As to Jesus, he too is about to come to the end of his own journey. The road from Gethsemane to Golgotha has been for him a long and painful road of complete expropriation. He had told his disciples, 'If any want to become my followers, let them deny themselves' (Mark 8:34). He showed the way, especially during his Passion: at Gethsemane, he lost his freedom, his disciples; during his trial before the Jewish and Roman authorities, he was deprived of his human dignity and of his reputation. On Golgotha, his clothes were taken away from him, and as he was about to lose this life, he wondered whether God had not gone away too. And it is that Jesus who now tells us again: 'Come, follow me.' Mark and Luke will guide us in our contemplation of Jesus at Calvary.

Jesus abandoned: Mark's story

'After mocking him, they stripped him of the purple cloak and put his own clothes on him. Then they led him out to crucify him... (Mark 15:21-41). It is important that before we start meditating on Jesus' death at Calvary, we take time to read the story Mark gives us of Jesus' last hours.

The Way of the Cross

We must be struck by the almost unbearable austerity of 'the way of the Cross' in Mark's gospel: just Jesus, led (the same verb could be translated 'carried') by four soldiers and Simon of Cyrene who carried the cross because he was forced to. In other words, we have here the group we would expect for the execution of any criminal.

And thus, Jesus' death will not be the honourable death of a prophet condemned to die for having defended God's honour to the end. Instead, it will be 'a numbing, squalid, tragic, grotesque, secular affair' [1] It was the miserable death of an ordinary criminal. We must even add, the miserable death of someone who dies 'cursed by the Law'. In the book of Deuteronomy, we read: 'When someone is convicted of a crime punishable by death and is executed, and you hang him on a tree [later this expression will be understood as applying also to crucified people], his corpse must not remain all night upon the tree; you shall bury him that same day, for anyone hung on a tree is under God's curse. You must not defile the land that the Lord your God is giving you for possession' (21:22-23).

Paul remembered this text when he wrote to the Christians of Galatia: 'Christ redeemed us from the curse of the law by becoming a curse for us–for it is written, "Cursed is everyone who hangs on a tree"' (3:13).

Jesus, on Calvary, was truly alone. In John's story of the Last Supper, Jesus had said to his disciples, 'The hour is coming, indeed it has come, when you will be scattered, each one to his home, and you will leave me alone. Yet I am not alone because the Father is with me' (16:32). But then, where was God, where was Abba on Calvary?

'My God, my God, why have you deserted me?'

Once again, we must remember how personal, how intimate was the relationship which bound Jesus to God. It was filled with immense trust, and therefore, Jesus' message was constantly filled with hope: 'do not be afraid, God, your Father, Abba, knows

---

1. Eamonn Bredin, *Disturbing the Peace*, p 212

and loves you.'

We are, therefore, all the more surprised, even shocked when we hear Jesus on the cross crying out, 'My God, my God, why have you deserted me?' (Mark 15:34).

These words are a quotation from Psalm 22, the prayer of a just, honest person oppressed, persecuted, crushed by enemies. The words uttered by Jesus are certainly the most desperate in the whole psalm, perhaps even in the whole Psalter. And now, Jesus addresses them to the God whom he calls 'Abba.' Jesus seems to have reached the ultimate frontier of distress, the line beyond which the human mind begins to sink, to undo itself.

It is important to realise that Jesus' last cry was, and is still uttered, in some way or other, by millions of men and women in the history of humankind: sick people, oppressed, tortured people, people dying of hunger. We think especially of the victims who died in concentration camps during the Second World War; people who experienced the absence of God. 'The time had gone when, as a child, you could hold out your hand to seize another hand, your mother's, the Law's, God's hand. Of course, you could, even now, hold out your hand, but it was in vain. All the victims of those years [the war years in the camps] had held out their hands until the last second: they had called, they had cried, they had prayed, under the gallows, under the axe, under torture. But no one had ever held those hands. Even in death, they remained stretched out, open, but withered, empty, alone'[2]

We must listen to Jesus' words, listen, listen, ... until we begin to hear!

The Mystery of God's absence on Calvary

We are still left with our question, where was God on Calvary? We find, in Mark's gospel (and also in the gospels of Matthew and Luke) two different, contrasting answers to this question. For Jesus' enemies, the answer was easy: God was obviously absent, unconcerned. If God had approved of Jesus, he would evidently have intervened in his favour: 'The chief priests, along

2. E. Wiechert, *Missa Sine Nomine*, Calmann Lévy, Paris 1953, p 70-71.
   (My own translation).

with the scribes were mocking him among themselves and saying, "He saved others; he cannot save himself"' (Mark 15:31-32).

Jesus' enemies are still more explicit in Matthew's gospel: 'He
trusts in God; let God deliver him now, if he wants to; for he
said, "I am God's Son"' (27:43).

Since God, the God of the Law, remained silent, it could only
mean that He did not approve of Jesus. On the evening of the
day when Jesus died, his enemies could say, 'Our God has won
the day.'

But for the Evangelists, for Christian faith, for Christian tradition, Calvary, contemplated in the light of Easter, is the great
hour when God's face was, at long last, 'unveiled', revealed. Mark,
together with Matthew and Luke, gives us two signs of the great
revelation of God on Calvary.

The Veil of the Temple

'Then Jesus gave a loud cry and breathed his last. And the curtain of the temple was torn in two, from top to bottom' (Mark
15:37-38)

There were two veils in the Temple sanctuary. The first veil
hid from view the first part of the sanctuary called 'the Holy'.
But there was another veil which separated 'the Holy' from 'the
Holy of Holies' where the Ark of the Covenant was, and on which
God's throne was situated. 'The Holy of Holies' was obviously
the most sacred place in the Temple of Jerusalem; there God
had chosen to dwell, 'my name shall be there' (I Kings 8:29).
But God's presence in the Holy of Holies was hidden; God's
throne was empty. Yet it was such a powerful symbol of the presence of God among his people that as the tradition of God's
People had it, no human being was allowed to cast his eyes on
God's empty throne; the empty throne was too much for human eyes to contemplate. So that, in the Temple sanctuary, God
was 'present' but unseen; God remained hidden.

In this context, Mark's words on 'the curtain of the Temple
being torn in two' contain a major theological affirmation: now
that Jesus has died on the Cross, the Temple veil has become
obsolete. If we want to have access to God, if we want to see God

with our own eyes, we must simply go up to Calvary and contemplate God's holy face revealed in Jesus: 'Who has seen me has seen the Father' (John 14:9).

The Centurion's Testimony

'Now when the centurion, who stood facing him, saw that in this way he breathed his last, he said, "Truly this man was God's Son!"' (Mark 15:39).

Traditionally, the centurion's words have been understood as a 'profession of faith.' A pagan, moved by what he has witnessed on Calvary, surrenders in faith to Jesus. Commissioned to execute a criminal, he now begins to realise that he has been drawn into the mystery of God unfolded in Jesus.

'You are my son, today I have fathered you'

St Paul can help us to go more deeply into that mystery. Speaking to the Jews of Antioch in Pisidia, Paul had this to say: 'We bring you the good news that what God promised to our ancestors he has fulfilled for us, their children, by raising Jesus; as also it is written in the second psalm, 'You are my Son; today I have begotten you' (Acts 13:32-33).

We find in these words of Paul an invitation to see Calvary in the light of Easter: Calvary is Easter in the making; Calvary is the supreme moment when God, the God of Life, the God who is 'father/mother' gives birth to Jesus again.

Perhaps the human experience of birth could allow us to draw nearer still to the awesome mystery of the relationship 'Abba-Jesus' as expressed on the Cross. In the birth of any human being, two 'passions' unfold: the 'passion' of the mother who experiences the birth of her child as the tearing away from her own body of the child whose home she has been for nine months; and the 'passion' of the baby who feels violently rejected by its mother in whose womb it felt so secure. And it is these two 'passions' which make possible the birth of a new life.

What light does this shed on Calvary? Where was God when Jesus was breathing his last? God was not 'up there', in the sky, commanding his son to die; nor was God present as a spectator.

On the contrary, God was fully involved, with infinite nearness and love, in the birthing of God's Son; Jesus felt as if God had abandoned him, deserted him, but God was, so to speak, in the depths of distress while his/her Son was being torn away from him/her. God was 'fathering/mothering his/her Son again': 'You are my Son, today I give you birth'. I like to see the presence of the women on Calvary as a symbol of the divine life-giving mystery' unfolding there.

'I came that they may have life and have it to the full' (John 10:10)

It was at Calvary, therefore, that God, 'the lover of life' (Wisdom 11:26) won a final victory over death. During his ministry, Jesus had come up against the forces of death at work in the world, and through his healing ministry, he had begun to give life, to heal life. But, of course, his life-giving action had been very limited; limited by time—his ministry lasted only three years, perhaps less; limited by space also—he had been sent only 'to the lost sheep of the House of Israel' (Matthew 15:24). It was limited, above all, by the human condition: all the people Jesus had healed, or even brought back to life, were destined to die some time later; death had the last word.

But the God whom Jesus had come to reveal could not be content with a limited, temporary victory. As St Irenaeus puts it, 'the glory of God is a human being fully alive.' Calvary was the supreme moment of God's final, complete victory: death itself was defeated; death in one of its ugliest forms, the death of a crucified man: 'You are my Son, today, I give you birth again.'

And therefore, now, life is radically changed. Whatever its wounds, by Abba's love, it will blossom into eternal life, 'for as all die in Adam, so all will be made alive in Christ (I Corinthians 15:22). As we contemplate Jesus in the deepest distress on the cross, we enter in faith into the mystery of his abandonment, and with him, we listen to the Father's voice: 'You are my child, today I given you birth.'

The Epiphany of God's Mercy: Luke's Story

Let us now turn to Luke's story of Jesus' final moments. 'As they led him away, they seized a man, Simon of Cyrene, who was coming from the country, and they laid the cross on him, and made him carry it behind Jesus…' (Luke 23:26-49).

As we have seen, Mark presented Jesus' death as 'the squalid, miserable death of an ordinary criminal' for whom no one seemed to have any sympathy, apart from some women who stood at a distance.

How different the picture given us by Luke. He too, like Mark, is aware that Jesus' death on the cross was brought about by hatred, and was a violent death. In his story, the leaders, the soldiers, and one of the criminals crucified with Jesus, express their feelings against Jesus.

But for Luke, what matters most is that Calvary was the out-pouring of God's mercy on the world; and in his story of Jesus' death, he shows us a great procession of people accompanying Jesus on his way to Golgotha, and being already embraced in the loving forgiveness flowing from the dying Jesus.

The way of the Cross was, for Mark, a most lonely experience for Jesus. Luke, on the contrary, sees Jesus accompanied by 'a great number of the people'; they did not seem to be against him, but 'they stood by, watching' on Golgotha, perhaps over-awed at seeing crucified the prophet from Nazareth; they will return home 'beating their breasts.'

In Mark's gospel, women were the only friendly but silent witnesses of Jesus' death, 'looking on, at a distance.' Luke asso-ciates them closely with Jesus' on his way to Calvary. There is between them and Jesus, a dialogue of mercy, the women 'beat-ing their breasts and wailing for him'; and Jesus expressing his great sorrow for them at the thought of what will happen to them when the Romans come, and besiege Jerusalem: 'Daugh-ters of Jerusalem, do not weep for me, but weep for yourselves and for your children' (Luke 23:27-28).

More striking still is the contrast between Jesus' last words in Mark's and in Luke's story:. In Mark, the only words spoken by Jesus express an immense distress: 'My God, my God, why have you deserted me?' In Luke, it is loving mercy which pours out of Jesus' heart: Jesus' words to the women on the way to Calvary; Jesus' words as he is being nailed to the cross: 'Father, forgive them, for they do not know what they are doing'; Jesus' words to the repentant thief: 'Today, you will be with me in Paradise.' And above all, Jesus' very last words, 'Father, into your hands, I commend my spirit.'

We must take our time, much time, to let Jesus' words of compassion and trust enter into our minds and hearts.

'When I am lifted up..., I will draw all to myself' (John 12:32).

We may presume that when Luke wrote his gospel, he was aware that there already existed passion stories, such as that found in Mark's gospel. Why then did he choose to rewrite the story of Jesus' passion and to give us so different a picture of Jesus at Calvary?

As a missionary who accompanied Paul on a number of his journeys, Luke knew how powerful the message of the cross had been to break open the boundary between Judaism and the early Christian communities. The cross, it is true, was perceived as folly by pagans, and as a scandal by the Jews; and yet, it had proved, since the beginning of the Christian mission, the very symbol of God's wisdom and power.

Truly, in the words of John the Evangelist, it was the cross which drew people to Jesus (12:32).

And that is what Luke seems to want to express in his story of Calvary. Luke's focus is not so much on 'what happened' on Calvary, but rather on what Calvary meant, what Calvary achieved. It began to bring people together: men and women, enemies and friends, Jews and pagans. One of the most striking expressions of Luke's aim in writing his passion story is the way he brings even Jesus' male disciples to Calvary. In Mark's and in Matthew's gospel, we are told that when Jesus was arrested in Gethsemane, 'all the disciples (the men) deserted him and ran away' (Mark 14:50). Luke omits this detail in his own version of Jesus' agony. But having brought 'a great number of people' to Golgotha, (different again from Matthew's and Mark's story') , he has also standing at a distance, together with the women who had followed Jesus from Galilee, 'all his acquaintances' (the Jerusalem Bible has, 'all his friends'), and the word 'acquaintances' is in the masculine. To Luke, it was obvious that all the disciples had to be on Calvary; and therefore, he brings them there.

At Calvary, in front of the crucified Jesus, we remember Jesus' words: 'Come, follow me, I will make you fishers of people.... If anyone has a mind to come after me, let them deny themselves, take up their cross and follow me.'

To follow the Jesus of Mark is to follow one who is abandoned, in solidarity with the poor, the sick, the lonely. To follow the Jesus of Luke, is to follow one who was sent to bring Good News to the Poor, the Good News of God's boundless mercy.

We must pray for love, the love which will give us the desire to contemplate Jesus crucified and to listen to his words. The love which will give us the strength to follow Jesus, and to be his witnesses in the world.

13

Jesus and Mary of Magdala
(*John 20:1-2, 11-18*)

On the evening of the day Jesus died, how did his disciples feel? We can easily imagine the men, huddled together in the Upper Room, ashamed of their cowardice at the moment of Jesus' arrest, afraid also of what might happen to them now if the Jewish authorities decided to crush every trace of the Jesus movement. For them, the journey of discipleship had abruptly come to an end: they were in the darkest possible night.

The women's situation was different. They had followed Jesus to Calvary, and when his body was finally put into a tomb, their minds were already made up: as soon as the sabbath was over, they would go back to the tomb, and mourn over Jesus, their master and friend.

The four gospels draw our attention to one of these women: Mary of Magdala, who was present on Calvary, and who, on the third day, early in the morning, went to the tomb (John 20:1). But whereas the gospels of Mark, Matthew and Luke show her together with other women, John singles her out and invites us to follow her in the pilgrimage which took her from the sorrow and darkness of Calvary and the tomb to the joyful light of Easter. 'Early on the first day of the week, while it was still dark, Mary Magdalen came to the tomb and saw that the stone had been removed from the tomb... Mary stood weeping outside the tomb...' (John 20:1-2,11-18).

Who was Mary of Magdala?

Mary was a disciple of Jesus. Luke tells us in his gospel that Jesus had met Mary of Magdala in Galilee: 'Soon afterwards he went on through cities and villages, proclaiming and bringing the good news of the kingdom of God. The twelve were with him, as well as some women who had been cured of evil spirits and infirmities: Mary, called Magdalen, from whom seven demons had gone out, and Joanna, the wife of Herod's steward Chuza, and Susanna, and many others, who provided for them out of their resources' (Luke 8:1-3).

Jesus had met Mary and healed her. Luke's text does not allow us to know whether Mary was just sick, though of an unusual form of sickness which people, therefore considered as Satan's work; or whether she was truly 'possessed.' But whatever her illness, Jesus had healed her. And from then on, together with other women, she was, as Luke puts it, 'with Jesus', and they 'looked after him' (Matthew 27-55).

A faithful disciple

Together with other women she followed Jesus to the end; it is striking that Mary is the only woman whose name is mentioned by the four gospels as being present on Calvary. Perhaps we should say that Mary was not only one of Jesus' faithful disciples, she was a friend of Jesus.

Mary of Magdala's experience of Jesus' death

Precisely because of the relationship which bound her to Jesus, his death was, for Mary, the end of a unique, marvellous experience which had transformed her life. Mary's yesterday, after Jesus had met her, had been so rich, so beautiful. And now it was all over.

And she could not have any hope that Jesus might rise soon from the dead. In the Judaism of Jesus' time, many Jews (among them the Pharisees) expected the just to rise at the end of time. But no one thought it possible for one just person to rise now.

And yet, there must have been in Mary something, — the love she had for Jesus — which refused to accept the finality of death. As the Song of Songs puts it, 'love is strong as death, passion fierce as the grave. Its flashes are flashes of fire, a raging flame. Many waters cannot quench love, neither can floods drown it' (8:6-7). Mary's journey towards Easter will be long, and difficult.

The Encounter on Easter morning

'Early on the first day of the week, while it was still dark, Mary Magdalen came to the tomb' (John 20:1).

Why did Mary go to the tomb on the morning of the Third Day? Mark and Luke show us the women going to the tomb in order 'to anoint Jesus' body' (Mark 16:1-2; Luke 24:1). Not so in John's gospel: according to John, the anointing of Jesus' body had already been performed by Joseph of Arimathaea and Nicodemus: 'They took the body of Jesus and wrapped it with the spices in linen cloths, according to the burial custom of the Jews' (John 19:40).

And so Mary went to the tomb, early on Easter morning, not to do something, but to be there. Because there, in the tomb, there was the body of Jesus, all that was left of Jesus, of the Jesus of Galilee, the Jesus Mary had followed and loved. To her, the body of Jesus was still the powerful symbol of her life yesterday, of the bond of friendship that bound her to Jesus. Near the tomb, Mary was as near as could be to the Jesus of yesterday.

The Drama of the Empty Tomb

When Mary discovered that 'the stone had been moved from the tomb' (John 21:1), she immediately ran to tell Peter and the disciple whom Jesus loved about it': 'They have taken the Lord out of the tomb, she said' (20:11). And she went back to the tomb: 'Mary was standing outside, near the tomb, weeping' (20:11).

What could Mary be waiting for, near the tomb, now that Jesus' body had disappeared? What did she want? Two questions, put to her by the other actors in the drama of the empty tomb, help her to express very clearly what she wants: to the angels' question, 'Woman, why are you weeping?' Mary answers: 'They have taken my Lord away, and I don't know where they have put him.'

The gardener who stands behind her goes further: 'Woman, why are you weeping', and he adds: 'who are you looking for?' It is essential that Mary be made aware of what she is looking for, of what she wants at all costs. And her answer is unequivocal:

'supposing him to be the gardener, she said to him, "Sir, if you have carried him away, tell me where you have laid him, and I will take him away"' (John 20:15). In other words, what Mary wants, what she is looking for, is Jesus' body, Jesus' corpse—the symbol of the marvellous experience which she had lived as a disciple of Jesus in the past, yesterday.

The great revelation

John highlights powerfully, and at the same time, with great gentleness, the tremendous mystery of the presence of the Risen Lord: 'Mary turned around and saw Jesus standing there, but she did not know that it was Jesus. Jesus said to her, "Woman, why are you weeping? Whom are you looking for?" Supposing him to be the gardener, she said to him, "Sir, if you have carried him away, tell me where you have laid him, and I will take him away"' (John 20:14-15).

'Jesus standing there': these, or similar words occur several times in the gospel Resurrection narratives: 'Jesus himself came up...' (Luke 24:15); 'Jesus came and stood among them (John 20:19); 'There stood Jesus on the shore' (John 21:14). Through these simple words, the Evangelists try to help us adjust our vision. The men and women who had accompanied Jesus during his ministry were obviously used to his presence and absence: one day he would be with them, another day he would be absent on some errand or other. But there is not, there cannot be, any succession of presence and absence for the Risen Lord: 'Risen', Jesus is there, always, our companion for ever: 'I am with you, yes, to the end of time' (Matthew 28:20).

Mary, however, must still be made aware of that. She is seeking the Jesus of yesterday, and since Jesus has died, she simply wants to have his corpse brought back to the tomb where she will in some way give it life again through the memory of her love. And Jesus is there, alive, near her, with her, 'now, here, now, always' (T.S.Elliot). But she does not, she cannot recognise him! And she will not, unless Jesus, the Risen Lord, draws her, raises her to the Easter reality.

'Mary...': the 'raising' of Mary begins with Jesus calling her name: a name which expresses for Jesus and Mary the unique relationship which binds them to each other: 'Do not be afraid, I have called you by your name, you are mine, you are precious in my eyes and I love you' (Isaiah 43:1,4).

'Do not cling to me.' Mary's reaction is immediate: she runs to Jesus and clings to him, as if she wanted to say: 'I lost you once, when you died on Calvary, I will not let you go away again.' Mary still thinks of the relationship which bound her to Jesus yesterday. And Jesus must open her eyes to the radical newness of the reality of his risen presence: 'do not cling to me because I have not yet ascended to the Father' (John 20,17). Now that Jesus is risen, there is no longer any past, or any future; there is only 'now', God's eternal now, this now which is given me: 'Surely, the Lord's mercies are not over, the Lord's deeds of faithful love are not exhausted; every morning they are renewed, great is the Lord's faithfulness' (Lamentations 3:22-23).

'The marvel of the moment', as Abraham Herschel puts it; the marvel of the 'now' filled to capacity by the Risen Lord's presence, the Lord calling us by our name, and inviting us to be fully open to the powerful living source of his love.

'Go to the brothers and tell them...' (John 20:17). As Mary enters hesitantly into the Easter world Jesus has just opened for her, Jesus entrusts her with a mission which will affirm, confirm her in her newly born Easter faith: 'Go to the brothers and tell them...' Mission will be, for Mary, the final healing touch given her by Jesus: 'Mary, do not think of yesterday; I am alive, your companion for ever. Go, proclaim the Good News; share with your brothers and sisters what you are experiencing now; do not keep anything for yourself; you will not lose what you will share; on the contrary, whatever you sow will bring to you unexpected fruits, the fruits of the love that binds you to me; you will become "a spring of living water" for the disciples' community.'

'And Mary of Magdala told the disciples: I have seen the Lord, and he has said these things to me' (John 20:18). Mary of Magdala, the first Easter missionary, the first bearer of the Good News the world had been waiting for since the beginning.

'Standing there is Jesus'

Mary's journey is also our journey, the journey of the Risen Lord's disciples. In our lives, just as in Mary's, 'standing there is Jesus', and therefore we are Easter disciples, and newness, growth, hope must be the hallmarks of our vision.

The Risen Lord calls us by our name, and invites us, as he invited Mary, to let go of all the corpses which may fill our hearts and our minds and prevent us from being open to 'the marvel of the moment.'

For we are not only the beneficiaries, but also, so often, the prisoners of our culture, of our experience, of our education, including our religious education. We easily think that we know. We cling to the images of God which fed the piety of our child-hood . We resent, or resist new ideas, new ways of thinking, of praying. We may feel that change threatens our security, and we oppose it. But the Spirit of the Risen Lord invites us to let our-selves be drawn into the movement of the 'new creation' which flows from the victory of life over death on Easter morning: Truly, 'the kindnesses of the Lord are not exhausted, they are renewed every morning' (Lamentations 3:22-23).

And of this hope we must be the standard bearers today in the world: 'Go and tell your brothers and sisters...'! Go and pro-claim that life is stronger than death, love stronger than hatred. 'Standing there, at the very heart of the ordinary in our daily lives, is Jesus the Risen Lord.'

14

The Road to Emmaus:
the Journey of Easter Faith
(*Luke 24:13-35*)

From the Cross to the Tomb: the end of the journey of discipleship?

'Joseph of Arimathaea bought a linen cloth, and taking down
the body of Jesus, wrapped it in the linen cloth, and laid it in a
tomb that had been hewn out of the rock. He then rolled a
stone against the door of the tomb' (Mark 15:46). ...And that,
seemingly, was the end of Jesus' journey, and therefore, the end
of the journey of discipleship: Jesus of Nazareth had called men
and women: 'Come, follow me.' Now that he was dead and bur-
ied, it was all over.

But on the third day, on Easter morning, startling news began to go round in Jerusalem: some women who had gone to
the tomb early in the morning, had come back and told the
other disciples that 'they had indeed seen a vision of angels who
said that he was alive' (Luke 24:23).

It had taken time for Mary of Magdala to let go of the fascina-
tion that Jesus' tomb had for her and to surrender to the evidence
of faith that Jesus was truly alive. It will take time for the Easter
faith to reach the hearts of all the disciples. That is a theme on
which Luke invites us to reflect at length in his story of the Road to
Emmaus.

On the Way to Emmaus: the Story of Journey

'Now on that same day two of them were going to a village called
Emmaus, about seven miles from Jerusalem, and talking with
each other about all these things that had happened. While they
were talking and discussing, Jesus himself came near and went
with them,...' (Luke 24:13-35).

More than in the other gospels, Jesus, in Luke's gospel, appears truly as 'a travelling Rabbi'; actually, Luke seems to consider the Good News of Jesus Christ as the sort of news which will inevitably draw people onto the roads: this is already remarkable in Luke's Infancy Narrative (Luke chapters 1 and 2) in which Luke has all the people involved in the drama of Jesus' birth constantly on the move, as if it were impossible to stay at home when such Good News is about to become reality. Remarkable also the long story of Jesus' journey to Jerusalem to which Luke gives ten chapters (Luke 9:51-19:27): 'As the time drew near for him to be taken up, Jesus resolutely turned his face towards Jerusalem' (9:51).

The Risen Lord, in the Emmaus story, remains true to Jesus of Nazareth: he takes to the road. A road which is first the road which leads from Jerusalem to Emmaus. But more deeply, a road which symbolizes the journey of the Easter faith. The journey which is also our journey.

The Women's Journey

Out of fidelity to the gospel Easter stories, one must distinguish between the women's Easter journey, and the men's.

The four gospels show us a group of women going to Jesus' tomb, early on the day following the Sabbath. This is how Luke tells the story: 'On the first day of the week, at early dawn, they came to the tomb, taking the spices that they had prepared. They found the stone rolled away from the tomb, but when they went in, they did not find the body. While they were perplexed about this, suddenly two men in dazzling clothes stood beside them. The women were terrified and bowed their faces to the ground, but the men said to them, "Why do you look for the living among the dead? He is not here, but has risen. Remember how he told you, while he was still in Galilee"' (Luke 24:3-6).

We must note the extraordinary contrast, in Luke's story, between the place where the women are, 'they went into the tomb', — that is, the place where death reigns supreme, the kingdom of death, the place where there is no hope —, and the message given them by the two men in dazzling clothes: 'Why do you look for the living among the dead? He is not here, but has risen'. The tremendous grace given to the women to hear the Good News that not even death can defeat life: Jesus is alive!

In Luke's story, the women immediately turn into heralds of this Good News: 'And returning from the tomb, they told all this to the eleven and to all the rest. Now it was Mary Magdalen, Joanna, Mary the mother of James, and the other women with them who told this to the apostles' (Luke 24:9-11).

We could say that the faultless fidelity with which the women had followed Jesus to Calvary blossomed into their faith in the Risen Lord; their journey as disciples became, by the power of Jesus' resurrection, an Easter journey. They were the first Easter missionaries, the missionaries of Jesus' victory of life over death.

The Men's Journey

The men's journey will prove long and difficult: 'Returning from the tomb, the women told all this to the eleven and to all the rest. Now it was Mary Magdalen, Joanna, Mary the mother of James, and the other women with them who told this to the apostles. But these words seemed to them an idle tale, and they did not believe them' (Luke 24:9-11).

Luke invites us to meet two of them who, on Easter day, left Jerusalem to go to a village called Emmaus: they did not see any point in staying in Jerusalem. They thought that Jesus of Nazareth, their Master, was the Messiah and they had hoped that 'he would be the one who would redeem Israel' (Luke 24:21). But their dreams crumbled lamentably when Jesus died on Calvary. Their distress was immense. They had better look for another road into a better future.

Where is the Risen Lord?

When the two men left Jerusalem, they were aware of the women's message, but it did not make sense. We can imagine the two travellers on the road to Emmaus amazed at the women's words, refusing to believe them, and yet, in some way, wondering.... If, as the women had proclaimed, Jesus was alive, where was he? The question which all disciples are bound to ask themselves, especially when there is darkness all around them, and there does not seem to be any light which would point to Easter.

The Risen Lord, our Companion on the Road

'Now on that same day two of them were going to a village called
Emmaus, about seven miles from Jerusalem, and talking with
each other about all these things that had happened. While they
were talking and discussing, Jesus himself came near and went
with them' (Luke 24:13-15).

Where is the Risen Lord? Where can the disciples, where can
we, find him? Luke's answer is: 'the Risen Lord is on the road
on which you are travelling now.' Luke's message echoes that of
the other Evangelists: the Risen Lord is wherever the disciples
are, whatever they may be doing: looking for Jesus' corpse; or just
'being together for fear of the Jews'; or again, fishing; or walking
on the road. And therefore, because Jesus is risen, all roads, all
places, all situations are Easter roads, and places, and situations.
We might not sense his presence, we might not be able to deci-
pher the signs of his presence but he is present, always.

In what capacity is the Risen Lord present to his disciples? As
the Lord, obviously, the Lord to whom 'all authority in heaven
and on earth has been given' (Matthew 28:18). Not, however,
as the Lord whose main concern would be to judge and condemn. The Risen Lord is 'their companion' (*cum pane*, the companion who shares his disciples' meals). He walks with them,
always taking them, accepting them as they are, without any precondition.

And the Risen Lord is their companion, our companion, for
their, for our sake. In Luke's story, it is striking that the Risen
Lord's sole concern is the wellbeing of the two men; at no moment does he try to draw their attention to himself; once again,
his sole concern is them, their distress, their journey, their experience. And because he is Risen, his very presence brings them
hope; their journey becomes an Easter journey.

An Easter Journey mapped out by the Scriptures

After having listened at length to the two men, the Risen Lord
takes over, so to speak. He must explain to them what the Easter

journey is about, how they will find their way: 'He said to them, "Oh, how foolish you are, and how slow of heart to believe all that the prophets have declared! Was it not necessary that the Messiah should suffer these things and then enter into his glory?" Then beginning with Moses and all the prophets, he interpreted to them the things about himself in all the scriptures' (Luke 24:25-27).

The link between the Scriptures and the distress of the two men might not be immediately apparent. It is however important that we should see it clearly.

What was the major problem which prevented the disciples from understanding Jesus, and from following him to the end? The two men on the road put it very simply: '...Jesus of Nazareth, who was a prophet mighty in deed and word before God and all the people, and how our chief priests and leaders handed him over to be condemned to death and crucified him. But we had hoped that he was the one to redeem Israel. Yes, and besides all this, it is now the third day since these things took place' (Luke 24:19-21).

Their major problem — the major problem with which all disciples are confronted — was the cross: the cross in all its forms, suffering, failure, death, any event, any situation which makes us wonder where God is, or whether God is really concerned about our happiness.

In his conversation with the two men on the way to Emmaus, the Risen Lord offered them the help of the Scriptures: 'He interpreted to them the things about himself in all the scriptures' (Luke 24:27).

How should we understand these words? The Scriptures are the record of the story of God's People; not the 'edifying story' of God's People, but the story of how they responded, or failed to respond to God's love for them; the story of God's dealings with God's People. They show us, again and again, that whatever the experiences of infidelity, of sin, of pain, of failure, of death which marked, and still mark, the journey of God's People, God never gives up, and in his loving providence, 'God cancels nothing but redeems all' (Dorothy Sayers). We would say today, recycles all; and the cross becomes, through God's love, the tree of life. Familiarity with the Scriptures can make us familiar with God's ways, and strengthen our faith and hope.

Provided, of course, we read the Scriptures in the light of the Risen Lord. Because he has travelled our roads, and knows and understands us, he alone can 'open our minds to understand the Scriptures' (Luke 24:45). He is 'the Word' in whom everything in the Scriptures falls into place. Perhaps should we pause a moment when we are about to read the Scriptures, and let the Risen Lord bearing the scars of his Passion enlighten our minds and hearts: 'In your light, we see the light' (Psalm 36:10).

Bread broken and shared

In Luke's story, the encounter between the two travellers and their companion reaches its climax in a meal: 'As they came near the village to which they were going, he walked ahead as if he were going on. But they urged him strongly, saying, "Stay with us, because it is almost evening and the day is now nearly over." So he went in to stay with them. When he was at the table with them, he took bread, blessed and broke it, and gave it to them. Then their eyes were opened, and they recognized him; and he vanished from their sight' (Luke 24:28-31).

The two travellers had not recognised Jesus in the stranger walking with them on the road to Emmaus. They had not recognised him either when he explained the Scriptures to them, though they admitted later that his words had set their hearts on fire (Luke 24:32). But now, at long last, their eyes were going to be opened; through a meal.

Why should a meal, a shared meal, reveal to them the true identity of their companion? If we are familiar with the gospels, we know how important shared meals were for Jesus: 'this man welcomes sinners and eats with them' (Luke 15:2). Meals were, for Jesus, moments when he offered healing to his table companions (Mark 2:15-17); meals were for him, 'sacraments' through which Abba's loving kindness reached out to people, without any preconditions, and made them whole. No wonder, therefore, if the 'breaking of bread' in the inn raised the two disciples out of the lethargy of their distress, and opened their hearts to the reality of Easter: 'their eyes were opened, and they recognised him' (Luke 24:31). They knew then that Jesus of Nazareth, who had died crucified on Golgotha, was truly alive, that he loved them, and offered them forgiveness, and healing. They were now, truly, Easter people.

And thus our Eucharist today, like yesterday, is for us the great Easter sacrament: the sacrament which fills our hearts with hope, because the Jesus who gave his life for us on the Cross has conquered hatred and violence, and pain, and failure, and even death, and he is our daily companion: 'In the word, you will have trouble, but be brave, I have conquered the world' (John 16:33).

The Easter Missionary Community

The two disciples' journey to Emmaus had been painful and slow. But all of a sudden, it gathers speed: 'That same hour they got up and returned to Jerusalem; and they found the eleven and their companions gathered together' (Luke 24:33).

The two men had left behind, in Jerusalem, the other disciples. But now that they had met the Risen Lord, they could not but go back to the community to which they belonged: discipleship is not, cannot be a lonely venture. How could we be authentic witnesses of the God who 'so loved us that he gave us his only Son' (John 3:16), if we want to go it alone. How could we be 'bread broken and shared' for the life of the world, if we want to eat our meals alone, and keep all the bread to ourselves. The community, the Christian community, our community must be, for us, the constant source of mutual inspiration, and support, and love; and it must be at the same time, the constant testing ground of the authenticity of our life as disciples.

Provided, of course, it be a 'missionary community', a community always willing, and anxious to share the hope given it by its faith in the Risen Lord.

A Journey filled with Hope

Truly, 'there is no waste with God, God cancels nothing but redeems all' The Risen Lord is for us the always flowing source of immense hope. As Paul puts it in his letter to the Christians of

Rome: 'If God is for us, who is against us? He who did not with-hold his own Son, but gave him up for all of us, will he not with him also give us everything else? If God is for us, who will bring any charge against God's elect?... It is Christ Jesus, who died, yes, who was raised, who is at the right hand of God, who indeed intercedes for us. Who will separate us from the love of Christ? Will hardship, or distress, or persecution, or famine, or naked-ness, or peril, or sword? ... No, in all these things we are more than conquerors through him who loved us. For I am convinced that neither death, nor life, nor angels, nor rulers, nor things present, nor things to come, nor powers, nor height, nor depth, nor anything else in all creation, will be able to separate us from the love of God in Christ Jesus our Lord' (Romans 8:33-39).

It is this hope that we, that I, must bring to the world today.

'Simon, son of Jonah, do you love me?'
(*John 21:1-19*)

'Why do you look for the living among the dead? He is not here, he has risen' (Luke 24:5). Jesus, the Risen Lord, is now your companion, on the road on which you are journeying, always. Go, therefore, and proclaim the Good News. Your journey is, must be, a journey filled with the spirit of Easter.

The Gospels of Matthew, Mark and Luke insist on the task of the disciples as they begin their Easter journey: 'Jesus came and said to them, "All authority in heaven and on earth has been given to me. Go therefore and make disciples of all nations, baptizing them in the name of the Father and of the Son and of the Holy Spirit, and teaching them to obey everything that I have commanded you' (Matthew 28:18-20).

John also sees the disciples' mission as finding its source in the Risen Lord. But as always, he puts a particular stress on the personal relationship which must bind the disciples to their Lord. That seems to be the central theme in the last story found in John's Gospel: 'the appearance on the shore of Lake Tiberias' (John 21:1-19)

Two types of Discipleship?

John's story singles out two disciples from among the seven who were on the Lake Shore when Jesus came to meet them: 'the disciple Jesus loved' and Peter.

The Disciple Jesus Loved

He is not given any name but he is referred to, here, as in the rest of the gospel, as 'the disciple whom Jesus loved': 'the disciple whom Jesus loved said to Peter...' (John 21:7). It is on him that the Evangelist focuses first his attention.

He is different from the other disciples, first through the name which he is constantly given; it is not an ordinary name, like Peter, or James by which are identified the people who wear those names. The expression, 'the disciple whom Jesus loved', identifies that disciple through the relationship which binds him to Jesus, as if that was enough to define him. And that is extraordinary.

He is different also through his great sensitivity to the Lord's presence: 'the disciple whom Jesus loved said to Peter, it is the Lord' (John 21: 7); the sensitivity of his love bound him to Jesus.

He is different again through his faultless fidelity to Jesus: he is mentioned for the first time during the Last Supper; or, at least, it is then that he is given his 'name' for the first time (John 13:13). We find him at the High Priest's palace during Jesus ' Jewish trial (John 18:15); and of course, at the foot of the cross on Calvary, together with Jesus' mother and other women (John 19:26). On Easter morning, he goes to the tomb with Peter after Mary of Magdala had found it empty, and he immediately begins to sense what had happened: 'He saw and believed' (John 20:8). In John's gospel, he seems to be considered as 'the first disciple', should we say, 'the perfect disciple.'

The name which he is given should not, however, lead us to conclude that the other disciples were not, are not loved, or loved as much by Jesus. We must say, on the contrary, that there is, in each one of us, 'the disciple whom Jesus loves', immensely. The disciple in us who is called to respond in love, faithfully; and whose sensitivity to the Lord's presence must enable him to say, 'It is the Lord.'

Simon Peter

The second disciple to be singled out by the Evangelist in the last story of his gospel is Simon Peter. Simon Peter was one of the first disciples to have been called by Jesus: 'Andrew first found his brother Simon and said to him, "We have found the Messiah." He brought Simon to Jesus, who looked at him and said, "You are Simon son of John. You are to be called Cephas"' (which is translated Peter) (John 1:41-42).

Peter was a born leader. He was no better than the other disciples, but there was something in him which prompted him to step forward, to speak in the name of the other disciples: 'Jesus asked the twelve, "Do you also wish to go away?" Simon Peter answered him, "Lord, to whom can we go? You have the words of eternal life"' (John 6:67-68).

But there was also the Peter of the Passion. In the high priest palace, to Caiaphas who was questioning Jesus about his disciples and about his teaching (John 18:19), Jesus answered: 'I have spoken openly to the world; I have always taught in synagogues and in the temple, where all the Jews come together. I have said nothing in secret. Why do you ask me? Ask those who heard what I said to them. They know what I said' (John 18:20-21).

At the same time, in the courtyard of the high priest's palace, 'Simon Peter was standing and warming himself. They asked him, "You are not also one of his disciples, are you?" He denied it and said, "I am not"' (John 18:25).

The shame it must have been for Peter! And after Jesus had died, he could not even ask Jesus to forgive him, it was too late. Peter had dreamt of a 'glorious passion' in which he would be faithful to the end to Jesus: 'I will lay down my life for you' (John 13:37); his 'passion', instead, was all humiliation and guilt, and remorse. He was then cornered into acknowledging his weakness, his misery, his distress.

The encounter on the Lake Shore

The Risen Lord is at the very heart of the ordinary in our daily lives. The face to face encounter between the Risen Lord and Simon Peter on the Lake Shore comes as the climax of a particularly rich and touching experience given to the seven disciples who had been fishing on the lake.

One should surely say that in his gospel, the fourth Evangelist puts a very strong stress on Jesus the Lord, on Jesus who, 'from the beginning was with God, was God.' The Jesus of the Fourth gospel is best represented by an icon on which, whatever he may be doing, he is enrobed in majesty; even the Passion story, in the fourth gospel, is filled with God's radiance; and the story of Calvary reads, in some way, as the solemn liturgy of the Birth of a new Human Race, Jesus being the majestic celebrant of that liturgy.

At the same time, however, John does not allow us to forget that 'the Word of God' was made flesh: and we think of Jesus at Cana, giving the wedding guests two hundred gallons of the best wine; we think of Jesus about to meet the Samaritan woman, and portrayed by the Evangelist as 'tired out by his journey, sitting by the well', and so thirsty (John 4:6); we think of Jesus, standing beside Lazarus' tomb, when he saw Mary weeping, and the Jews who came with her also weeping, Jesus 'was greatly disturbed and deeply moved..., and he began to weep' (John 11:33-35).

It is this same profoundly human Jesus who appears to the disciples on the lake shore after Easter. I marvel at the Risen Lord, standing on the shore, and asking the men fishing from the boat on the Lake, 'Children, you have no fish, have you?' And then, to the fishermen admitting that they have worked the whole night, but for nothing, Jesus, the Risen Lord gives a useful hint, 'Cast the net to the right side of the boat, and you will find some' (John 21:5-6). 'Some...', that is, actually, 'a hundred and fifty large fish' (John 21:11); a catch far beyond anything the fishermen could have hoped for! And finally, the last words from the Risen Lord to his disciples in John's gospel, before he met Peter face to face: 'Come and have breakfast' (John 21:12). Truly, yes, the Risen Lord, 'God from God, light from light, true God from true God', as the Nicene Creed will put it later; but also truly fully one of us, present at the very heart of the ordinary in our lives, interested in, concerned about whatever makes up our daily lives. We remember St Irenaeus' words: 'the glory of God is a human being fully alive.'

Jesus and Peter face to face

'Simon, son of John, do you love me?' (John 21:15,16,17). Jesus' threefold question to Peter is obviously meant to match Peter's threefold denial during the Passion. We might be tempted to think that in a way, it was the wrong question to put to Peter who, a few days, or hours earlier, had emphatically denied that he was one of Jesus' disciples. We would rather have expected Jesus to tell Peter: 'after what has happened in the high priest's courtyard, I have decided to entrust to someone else the leadership of the Twelve.' We ourselves so easily and frequently label people with the mistakes they have made, the faults they may have committed: 'Peter, the man who denied his master', or as the gospels themselves always write, 'Judas, the man who betrayed Jesus'; as if Peter was for ever identified with the moment when he denied Jesus, or Judas with the moment he betrayed Jesus.

But that is not the way Jesus sees people: he knows us, he knows how weak, how sinful, how vulnerable we are; he also knows the love, the generosity, the good will the Father has put into our hearts; he knows that these gifts from the Father co-exist with our weakness, our sinfulness, our vulnerability: we are not, at any time, just bad; we can be, at the same time, both faithful and unfaithful, loving and non-loving. And therefore, Jesus sees us with an immense love and mercy. He looks at us in order to renew us, to confirm, to affirm us.

'Lord, you know that I love you': Peter sensed that Jesus' question was not meant as a roundabout way of condemning him for his threefold denial; he sensed that Jesus knew, that even when he was denying him, he was still in love with him.

Peter's answer to Jesus' question is filled with humility. We can imagine that to a similar question put to him by Jesus before the Passion, Peter would have answered: 'Of course, Lord, I love you.' He was then so sure of himself: 'I will never disown you!'. But now, he leaves it to Jesus because Jesus does know, and Jesus' knowledge springs from his heart: 'Lord, you know that I love you.' Peter's humble answer shows the genuineness of his love for Jesus.

'Feed my lambs, feed my sheep' (John 21:15,16,17). Where we would have expected Peter to be demoted from his position as head of the Twelve, Jesus confirms him in his mission: 'Simon, son of John, do you love me? Yes, Lord, you know that I love you. Feed my lambs, feed my sheep', that is, 'take care of the community of my disciples.' I find these words extraordinary, filled with Jesus' love for Peter, and his trust in someone who is in no way a saint, or a hero: 'You love me, therefore, take care of the community', that will be the only fully valid test of the genuineness of Peter's love for Jesus. It was true of Peter, it is true of each one of us.

And we must even go further and say that actually, Peter is now better equipped to fulfil his mission. Now that he is aware of his own vulnerability, of his weakness, of his sinfulness, he will find it easier to understand people, to forgive and affirm them.

We find a somewhat similar face to face between Jesus and Peter in Luke's version of the Last Supper: 'Simon, Simon, listen! Satan has demanded to sift all of you like wheat, but I have prayed for you that your own faith may not fail; and you, when once you have turned back, strengthen your brothers' (Luke 22:31-32).

We have here, both in Luke's and in John's gospel, words of the Risen Lord to his disciples which spell out powerfully, beautifully, what Easter means as we continue our journey as disciples: Easter means that Jesus the Risen Lord does not linger and does not want us to linger, on our infidelities. Conversion does not consist in dwelling on in our past, but rather in turning away from ourselves, and letting the loving mercy of the Risen Lord open our hearts and minds, our lives to people, to everyone, beginning with our community. That is what the new life flowing from the Risen Lord is about. And through the power of his love, our weaknesses, and sins are 'the cracks through which the light comes in' (Leonard Cohen).

Peter's Journey

In the early Church, Peter played the role given him by the Risen Lord: he fed the flock entrusted to him. It was not an easy task. We know in particular that at times, he had problems with Paul's approach to the apostolic ministry. Paul gives us his own version of an incident which took place at Antioch in Syria and which involved Paul himself and Peter; Paul was certainly convinced that Peter was wrong, and he told him so in no uncertain terms (see Galatians 2:11-14). Yet we wonder whether it was not Peter who, patiently and humbly, helped Jewish Christians and Christians of pagan origin to accept and respect one another, and to live together in the same communities.

And thus, Peter's journey went on. He had had to learn, as he followed Jesus of Nazareth, to let go of his own will 'to run the show' in his own way. As he moved on in life, and in his apostolic ministry, he had to let go, again and again, of his own plans: 'Very truly, I tell you, when you were younger, you used to fasten your own belt and to go wherever you wished. But when you grow old, you will stretch out your hands, and someone else will fasten a belt around you and take you where you do not wish to go. (He said this to indicate the kind of death by which he would glorify God) (John 21:18-19).

His journey finally took him to martyrdom: the moment came when, like Jesus, he had to let go of his freedom, and of his own life, and once again, and this time for ever, he found himself face to face with Jesus, the Risen Lord, whom he had loved, and served, humbly, faithfully. I love to see in the following passage from the first letter attributed to Peter, an echo of Peter's deepest longing: 'Blessed be the God and Father of our Lord Jesus Christ. By his great mercy he has given us a new birth into a living hope through the resurrection of Jesus Christ from the dead, and into an inheritance that is imperishable, undefiled, and unfading, kept in heaven for you... In this you rejoice, even if now for a little while you have had to suffer various trials... Although you have not seen him, you love him; and even though you do not see him now, you believe in him and rejoice with an indescribable and glorious joy, for you are receiving the outcome of your faith, the salvation of your souls' (1 Peter 1:3-9).

One word sums it all up: the word which Peter had heard first in Galilee, when Jesus called him; the word which the Risen Lord repeated to him on the Lake shore; the word which, in some way, gives us the essential of our call, of our lives: 'After this he said to him, "Follow me"' (John 21:18-19).

16

Pentecost

'Go into the whole world and proclaim the Good News'
(Matthew 28:19)

All the Easter stories in the gospels are, in some way or other, 'Mission stories': 'Go and tell my brothers and sisters...' (John 20:17). If Jesus is risen, then, there must be mission: 'All authority has been given me in heaven and earth, go therefore and make disciples of all nations' (Matthew 28:19).

The New Testament offers us a variety of approaches to the mission entrusted by Jesus to his disciples; a variety which reflects 'the boundless riches of Christ' (see Ephesians 3:8); a variety which is also, for us, an invitation to welcome, to be open to the Spirit's message for us today.

We will take as our guide St Luke who is the author of both the third gospel and the Acts of the Apostles. Luke was of Greek origin, a convert from paganism. For many years, he was a companion of Paul in his missionary journeys. Two experiences in particular seem to have impressed Luke and shaped his vision of mission: first, the experience of the development of Christianity. From Jerusalem, it had already spread in Luke's own time in fulfilment of the Risen Lord's promise, 'to the ends of the earth': 'You will receive power when the Holy Spirit has come upon you; and you will be my witnesses in Jerusalem, in all Judea and Samaria, and to the ends of the earth' (Acts 1:8).

There was also Luke's experience of the importance of Christian communities – the communities where tradition was kept, where the liturgy was celebrated; where 'communion' was not just a word, but could and did take flesh.

And to Luke, that was the work of the Holy Spirit, as the Acts of the Apostles show. It was the Spirit promised by the Risen Lord to his disciples: 'You will receive power when the Holy Spirit has come upon you' (Acts 1:8); the same Spirit whom Luke perceives as the inner power who gives the disciples the courage and audacity to bear witness to the gospel: 'We cannot stop proclaiming what we have seen and heard' (Acts 4:20); the Spirit who brings the disciples to open up their communities to all peoples.

Let us now focus our attention on Luke's story of Pentecost in Jerusalem: Acts 2:1-12. Luke sets the experience of the coming of the Spirit on Jesus' disciples within the context of the Jewish feast of Pentecost. What does this mean?

The Jewish feast of Pentecost

Originally, the feast of Pentecost was for the Israelites a harvest festival, the feast of the first-fruits of the grain harvest (Exodus 23:14-17). Later, it was integrated into the 'sacred history' of God's People and became the feast of the gift of the Law by God to Moses on Mount Sinai.

The Law, God's Law, played a major role in shaping the history and the spirituality of Israel. Yet, it was so often forgotten, or misused by the Israelites that prophet Jeremiah, and prophet Ezekiel expressed the hope that one day, God would step in again into the life of God's People and offer them a new covenant accompanied by a new Law:

'The days are surely coming, says the Lord, when I will make a new covenant with the house of Israel and the house of Judah....This is the covenant that I will make with the house of Israel after those days, says the Lord: I will put my law within them, and I will write it on their hearts; and I will be their God, and they shall be my people' (Jeremiah 31:31-34).

'I will take you from the nations, and gather you from all the countries, and bring you into your own land....A new heart I will give you, and a new spirit I will put within you; and I will remove from your body the heart of stone and give you a heart of flesh. I will put my spirit within you, and make you follow my statutes and be careful to observe my ordinances' (Ezekiel 36:24-27).

The Christian Feast of Pentecost

It was on the feast of the Jewish Pentecost that, according to

Luke, the Spirit came on the disciples gathered together in the Upper Room in Jerusalem. For Luke, therefore, this event marked the fulfilment of the promise made by God through the prophets. It was the Spirit, the Holy Spirit sent from the Father by the Risen Lord who would, now, guide the community of God's People born of Easter: 'a new Spirit, a new heart, a heart of flesh...'

There is matter here for reflection and prayer: 'a new spirit, a new heart, a heart of flesh'... Fidelity to the Law of the New Covenant, to God's will, is not, should not be just compliance with a rule, a law, out there, outside me; like road signs telling me which way I should go to reach my destination, but without giving me the energy to journey on. Instead, 'a new law' written on our hearts, an inner impulse, the impulse of love moving us in the way of God's will. St Thomas Aquinas speaks of the love which has been poured into our hearts (Romans 5:5) and is, in our hearts, like a weight which makes us lean instinctively, so to speak – the instinct of the Spirit within us – towards God, *pondus amoris*, as Thomas Aquinas puts it. Obedience then ceases to be a burden to become a loving demand of love.

Luke's story, however, draws our attention to another aspect of the experience given to the disciples at Pentecost: an aspect which was particularly dear to Luke the missionary. Luke knew, and so did many other people in the early Christian communities, how difficult it had been, and it remained, to bring together, through the preaching of the Good News of Jesus Christ, converts from Judaism and converts from paganism. The Acts of the Apostles give us several stories of incidents which opposed to each other members of both groups, and even some of the major leaders of the Christian communities such as Peter and Paul (see Acts 15; Galatians 2:11-14). Yet, Luke believed that, through it all, the Holy Spirit kept on guiding the leading witnesses and their communities towards openness to cultures, and races, and towards the freedom of the gospel.

'They were all filled with the Holy Spirit...'

Let us read again and comment on Luke's story: 'And suddenly from heaven there came a sound like the rush of a violent wind,

and it filled the entire house where they were sitting.' (Acts 2:2).
In order to help us approach the mystery of the Holy Spirit
coming to the disciples, Luke makes use of the symbols found
in the Old Testament to 'describe' the experience which God's
People had of the active presence of God in their lives.

'The rush of a violent wind.' The very name of the Spirit makes
us think of 'wind', of 'breath.' And we remember 'God's spirit
(wind, or breath) which hovered over the water' from which,
through God's Word, sprang up the universe (Genesis 1:1); we
remember the breath of life given by God to the first human
being (Genesis 2:7); we remember the 'spirit/breath' of God
raising back to life the dry bones of God's People (Ezekiel 37:1-
14); we remember the 'Spirit' of new birth offered by Jesus to
Nicodemus: 'Very truly, I tell you, no one can enter the kingdom of God without being born of water and Spirit. What is
born of the flesh is flesh, and what is born of the Spirit is spirit.
Do not be astonished that I said to you, "You must be born from
above." The wind blows where it chooses, and you hear the sound
of it, but you do not know where it comes from or where it goes.
So it is with everyone who is born of the Spirit' (John 3:5-8).

The Spirit brings the newness, the imagination, the creativity at work in Jesus' resurrection; the newness, the imagination,
the creativity of love. It is the Spirit who comes unexpectedly,
and so often, therefore, disturbs us; the Spirit who, at times, is
'gentle breeze' (I Kings 19:12-13), a 'breath of fresh air' in our
lives, in the life of the Church, in the life of our communities;
but also the Spirit who can be like a hurricane which sweeps our
hearts, our minds, our lives free from so much refuse accumu-
lated over the years.

'Divided tongues ... appeared among them...'

The Jerusalem Bible puts it, 'Something appeared to them that
seemed like tongues of fire': and we must think immediately of
'language', 'communication', the power to speak, to communicate, and therefore, to enter into 'communion' with others. We
sense, here, the vivid and rich experience of Luke, the missionary, Paul's companion, and of course, before Paul, the experi-

ence of Jesus whom John will call later, 'the Word': 'In the beginning, the Word was with God, and the Word was God' (John 1:1).
The mission of the apostles, the disciples will be 'communication',
it will aim at 'communicating' the Good News of Jesus Christ.

'Tongues of fire...'

John the Baptist had announced that 'he who was to come after
him' would give a baptism of 'spirit and fire', and John had in
mind the 'judgement' brought about by the Messiah's mission.
Jesus did not bring God's judgement to the world, but rather
'the year of God's favour.' His was the fire of love: 'I have come to
bring fire to the earth, and how I wish it were blazing already' (Luke
12:49). The Spirit of Pentecost will give the apostles, the disciples to
speak the language of love, to proclaim the Good News of 'the God
who loved the world so much that he gave his only Son' (John
3:16).

'Filled with the Holy Spirit, they began to speak in other languages'

Luke's story of Pentecost in the Acts of the Apostles is very much
focused on 'the Good News being communicated', proclaimed by
the Apostles filled with the Holy Spirit. We must linger on this
aspect of the mystery of the Church, the mystery of our Christian
faith.

The apostles were gathered together in the Upper Room, 'for
fear of the Jews', as John puts it (John 20:19). Luke puts it more
positively showing them 'in continuous prayer' (Acts 1:16). But
whatever the reason for their being together, they were certainly
not busy proclaiming any message to the world. It was the Holy
Spirit who prompted them to go out and preach with great as-
surance 'God's deeds of power', or, as the Jerusalem Bible puts
it, 'the marvels of God' (Acts 2:12).

Note the dominant vocabulary in Luke's story: it is all about
'speaking and hearing.' Pentecost shows us the Spirit as the 'Go-
between God' who constantly invites us to go out of ourselves in
order to speak, to communicate, to share the Good News of
Jesus, and thus to bring people together in the communion of
faith.

'A miracle of communication', Pentecost is also, in Luke's story, the miracle of 'unity, of at-oneness' in the making. There were people 'from every nation under heaven' (Acts 2:5) in Jerusalem, in the crowd listening to the apostles; and 'each one of them heard them (the apostles) speaking in the native language of each: '... in our own languages,' they said, 'we hear them speaking about God's deeds of power' (Acts 2:6,11).

And the miracle of Pentecost goes on: the Spirit calls us all to be bridge-builders, community-makers, through sharing the Good News of Jesus Christ which has been entrusted to us. We must, therefore, – it is a demand made on us by our faith – be willing and ready to speak out, to communicate, and therefore to accept the risk entailed in speaking, in communicating; the risk entailed in coming out of the security of silence.

We must be willing and ready to speak out, to communicate 'the marvels of God', the 'Good News of Jesus-Christ', and to do it in such a way that the 'Good News' is perceived, 'perceivable' as 'Good News' by the people who hear it. Or, as Christophe Theobald, a German theologian, puts it, we must, as we speak out, as we communicate the 'Good News', make the gospel 'desirable.'

We must be willing and ready to speak out, to communicate the 'marvels of God', 'the Good News', not as something casual, but as the 'Good News' which has become our life, our passion.

We must be willing and ready to speak out, to communicate the 'marvels of God', 'the Good News, in such a way that people can understand and feel invited to take a decision which will transform their lives.

We must let these words and images challenge us. Entrusted with the 'Good News' of Jesus Christ, do we try not only to let it guide and inspire our own lives, but 'communicate it'? If it is for me, truly, 'Good News', then surely I must be keen on sharing it, in some way or other, with the people I live with, the people I meet. If I don't, if I don't feel the urge to communicate the gift of faith which I have received, what is the reason? Perhaps I may need to become more aware of the value of the treasure which has been given me? Perhaps I need to listen more attentively, more lovingly to Jesus' call inviting me to be a witness of the gospel today in the world.

'United, heart and soul'

Luke concludes his Pentecost story with a description of the first Christian community in Jerusalem; a description which we might consider as over-optimistic (there were problems, real problems among the first Christians!), but a description which shows us very clearly what the proclamation of the Good News of Jesus Christ must lead to. 'They devoted themselves to the apostles' teaching and fellowship, to the breaking of bread and the prayers. Awe came upon everyone, because many wonders and signs were being done by the apostles. All who believed were together and had all things in common; they would sell their possessions and goods and distribute the proceeds to all, as any had need. Day by day, as they spent much time together in the temple, they broke bread at home and ate their food with glad and generous hearts, praising God and having the goodwill of all the people. And day by day the Lord added to their number those who were being saved' (Acts 2:42-47).

The stress is clearly on 'community, at-oneness', in conformity with Jesus' constant insistence on charity, forgiveness, unity. We are, all of us, the daughters and sons of the God who is love, our Abba.

A community of faith gathered together by the Apostles' message: the message to which we must constantly go back because it is the source of our faith.

A community of hope, for we are all on our way to the Father.

A community of love, brothers and sisters, united, heart and soul, brought and kept together by the breaking of bread and sharing their gifts with one another. Luke puts a special stress on this sharing: 'All who believed were together and had all things in common; they would sell their possessions and goods and distribute the proceeds to all, as any had need... The whole group of those who believed were of one heart and soul, and no one claimed private ownership of any possessions, but everything they owned was held in common.... There was not a needy person among them, for as many as owned lands or houses sold them and brought the proceeds of what was sold. They laid it at the apostles' feet, and it was distributed to each as any had need. (Acts 2:44-45;4:32-35).

Luke's insistence may be due to his own experience as a missionary. He must have seen, again and again, in his travels, how difficult it was, even for the first Christians, to share with one another, to share their faith, to share also their goods. Paul, writing to the Christians of Corinth, protested, as we have already seen, at the way in which they, in the very celebration of the Lord's Supper, 'showed contempt for the church of God and humiliated those who had nothing' (I Corinthians 11:22).

A praying community was not just a community of 'people who prayed', but a community of people who prayed together 'They devoted themselves to the apostles' teaching and fellowship, to the breaking of bread and the prayers... Day by day, they spent much time together in the temple' (Acts 2:42,46). And the 'breaking of bread' (one of the very first names given to the Eucharist), must have been for them the all-important moment when they remembered Jesus and heard anew his invitation: 'Do this in memory of me', 'be ready to be bread broken and shared' for others, especially the poor.

The story of Pentecost is not just a beautiful story of an event which took place long ago. It is, it must be, the story of the Church, the story of all Christian communities, in which the Spirit of the Risen Lord is present and active, and invites us 'to be of the same mind as Christ Jesus' (Philippians 2:5). We have been reflecting at length on 'the Journey of discipleship.' The event of Pentecost assures us that as we seek to journey on, with Jesus, the Holy Spirit accompanies us and urges us never to lose sight of our call: to be witnesses of the Good News of Jesus Christ in the world today, to be witnesses together, as communities bound by the bond of love; to be witnesses who 'cannot stop proclaiming what they have seen and heard', the Good News of Jesus Christ, our Lord, and Saviour, and brother.

17

Food for the Journey
'Do this in memory of me'
(*Luke 22:19*)

The last few hours Jesus spent with his disciples before he entered into his Passion were spent sharing a meal with them. His last meal. A meal whose importance and uniqueness is brought out in the gospels. A meal in which Christian tradition sees the founding experience of the sacraments of Holy Orders and of the Eucharist.

And actually, as we know, it was in the course of that last meal that Jesus, taking bread into his hands, thanked God for it, broke it and gave it to his disciples, saying, 'This is my Body, which is for you, do this in memory of me' (Luke 22:19).

But what is the meaning of these founding words of Jesus', 'Do this in memory of me?' What could they mean for the disciples in the Upper Room? What do they mean for us today?

We could be content with answering, 'to do this in memory of Jesus' is an invitation of Jesus to repeat what he did at the Last Supper; to repeat his words and gestures. But surely, that is not enough. Jesus wants to invite his disciples to go far beyond the ritual words and gestures: 'live up to what you are doing and saying.' Jesus' words and gestures over the bread and wine at the Last Supper are for us in some way the programme of our lives as disciples of Jesus. We must spend time reflecting and praying over the immense riches of the eucharist. We will discover that the eucharist, 'the Lord's Supper', as Paul calls it (I Corinthians 11:20), sums up Jesus' life, and ministry, and Passover, and for us, 'the journey of discipleship.'

'This man welcomes sinners and eats with them' (Luke 15:2)

Jesus' words, 'do this in memory of me', obviously send us back to the gospel accounts of the Last Supper, the accounts which have been a constant source of inspiration for theology, spirituality and Christian art. But we must not forget that the 'Last' Supper was precisely the last of a whole series of suppers that Jesus shared with his own and with others. And it is to Jesus' meals that we must go back to recapture the fulness of meaning of the Last Supper and of the Eucharist, and face their challenge. The Eucharist is the sacrament of Jesus' Passover, of Jesus' sacrifice, yes, beyond any doubt. But it is also a meal. And Jesus' table-companionship will be the angle from which we will reflect on the Eucharist.

'You are my Son, the Beloved, with you I am well pleased'

At the source, as always, there was Jesus' experience at the Jordan some time before he launched into his public ministry: 'Just as he was coming up out of the water, he saw the heavens torn apart and the Spirit descending like a dove on him. And a voice came from heaven, "You are my Son, the Beloved; with you I am well pleased."' (Mark 1:10-11).

Jesus was confirmed in the unique relationship which bound him to God, the God he called 'Abba.' Consequently, his ministry consisted simply in living out the message received at the Jordan; in making 'Abba', Abba's Kingdom, become 'Good News' to people, become reality in the lives of the poor.

And so, the source of it all, the source to which we must always go back if we want to understand the wealth of meaning of everything in Jesus' person, life and ministry, is the immense kindness of the God whom Jesus had come to reveal to the world. As John puts it, 'No one has ever seen God, but the only Son who is close to the Father's heart, he has made him known. (John 1:18).

'He took our infirmities and bore our diseases' (Matthew 8:17)

How did Jesus go about fulfilling his mission? One of the major activities in Jesus' ministry, according to the gospels of Matthew, Mark and Luke, was his healing ministry: 'He had cured many, so that all who had diseases pressed upon him to touch him' (Mark 3:10).

Through spending so much time with the sick, through healing them, Jesus made the Good News of Abba's kingdom begin to become reality in their lives.

'When Jesus was at dinner in Levi's house...' (Mark 2:15)

But the gospels also draw our attention to another activity of Jesus' which we have tended to overlook: Jesus' meals. Eamonn Bredin puts it beautifully: 'In reading the gospels, we might be forgiven for thinking that Jesus is always coming from, going to, or talking about banquets, feasts and meals. He is remembered vividly as a companion at table, as someone to whom meals were very important. Opponents coined a catch-call and flung it at him: 'Look, a glutton and a drunkard, a friend of tax-collectors and sinners.' [1]

And actually, leafing through the gospels, we will have to agree with Eamonn Bredin: meals were very important to Jesus. They were an essential aspect of his ministry, a 'work' through which Jesus expressed his person, his mission, and made the Kingdom 'happen', the Kingdom of the Father's merciful kindness: 'this man welcomes sinners and eats with them' (Luke 15:2) – because God is like that.

But why did Jesus attach so much importance to the meals he shared with people?

He was seen at table with all sorts of people: with his disciples, of course, and with friends like Martha and Mary in Bethany (Luke 1à:38-42); but also with Pharisees and Lawyers (see Luke 14:1-14). But it was the marginalised, people considered as 'sinners', who were Jesus' privileged table-companions.

Jesus' attitude was all the more striking as Jewish society at that time was very strict in the practice of table hospitality. Meals, especially festive meals, were for them Covenant celebrations; that is, privileged moments when members of the Covenant community came together to share with one another the fruits of the Covenant land: 'Blessed are you, Lord, God of all creation, through your goodness, we have this bread to offer...' A shared meal expressed, celebrated and strengthened the Covenant bond of the Covenant community.

Moments of communion between the members of the Covenant community, shared meals were also moments from which

---

1. Eamonn Bredin, *Disturbing the Peace*, Columba Press, 1985, Dublin, p 134

pagans were excluded; not only pagans, but also 'sinners', that is, Jews who because of their profession, because of the way they lived, were considered as being outside the Covenant community.

In other words, for good, practising Jews, shared meals were both moments of communion for the 'in-group', and moments of discrimination against others.

In this context, Jesus' attitude could not but surprise, and even scandalise many people: 'this man welcomes sinners and eats with them' (Luke 15:2); 'the Son of Man came, eating and drinking, and they say, Look, a glutton and a drunkard, a friend of tax-collectors and sinners' (Matthew 11:19).

Why did Jesus choose to go against the practise of his own people? What was the meaning of the meals he shared with people? What did he expect from them? Jesus himself was given by his opponents an opportunity to explain his own attitude: 'As Jesus was walking along, he saw a man called Matthew sitting at the tax booth; and he said to him, "Follow me." And he got up and followed him. And as he sat at dinner in the house, many tax collectors and sinners came and were sitting with him and his disciples. When the Pharisees saw this, they said to his disciples, "Why does your teacher eat with tax collectors and sinners?" But when he heard this, he said, "Those who are well have no need of a physician, but those who are sick. Go and learn what this means, 'I desire mercy, not sacrifice.' For I have come to call not the righteous but sinners"' (Matthew 9:9-13).

Thus, to Jesus, shared meals were meant to be experiences of healing for people who sat at his table. But how could a meal shared with 'tax-collectors and sinners' allow Jesus to offer them healing? These people were marginalised in Jewish society; good, practising Jews kept away from them. But Jesus accepted them, offered them respect, and welcome, and communion, without any precondition, and through sharing with them the companionship of a meal, he made the Kingdom of God begin to become reality for them. Table-companionship was, for Jesus, the sacrament of God's immense merciful kindness for people. Obviously, a meal shared with Jesus did not change immediately and thoroughly tax-collectors and sinners into saints. But it started them on the road to discipleship: having met Jesus, and shared a meal with him, tax-collectors and sinners now knew that there was, in Israel, a man of God, Jesus, and a community around him, a community where they had been accepted, respected, and where they knew they would always be welcomed. They had been given a taste of the Kingdom of God, a taste of the healing they longed for.

We must keep all this in mind when we reflect on the Last Supper, and on the Eucharist: we are already able to understand why the last hours Jesus could spend with his disciples before his Passion began, were spent sharing a meal with them. To Jesus, it was in some way essential that it be so. Let us now focus our attention on the Last Supper.

'They were at supper...' (John 13:2)

Whatever their individual approach, the four Evangelists agree that the Last Supper was a meal; a meal where the people present ate and drank; but also shared with one another their thoughts, their feelings; Luke even mentions a discussion the disciples had over 'who was the greatest' (Luke 22:24-27). It was a shared meal filled with the richness of table-companionship. But even as a meal like so many other meals shared by Jesus and his disciples, the atmosphere of this 'Last Supper' was permeated by the threat which now weighed down on Jesus. Jesus knew his enemies were about to put their hands on him, and therefore, his words, his gestures, all had a finality about them which one feels when reading the Evangelists' story. A meal, but also the last meal...

And we must add, 'a meal with sinners': Judas was there, although he had already decided to betray Jesus; Peter was there, full of good will, and yet so vulnerable; another few hours and he would say about Jesus, in the courtyard of the high-priest's palace, 'I do not know the man'; other disciples who seemed to be more concerned about their place in the disciples' group than about the threat which hung over Jesus; within a few hours, they too will, in Mark's words, 'desert Jesus and run away' (14:50). Jesus knew them all, he knew how weak they were; but it was their very weakness and sinfulness which made it essential for him to share with them, without any precondition, the healing experience of a last meal. He wanted to assure them that whatever happened, he would love them, he would be faithful to the friendship that bound them to himself and to one another. He wanted to assure them that there would be open to them a fountain of forgiveness from which they could always draw: 'Simon, Simon, listen! Satan has demanded to sift all of you like wheat, but I have prayed for you that your own faith may not fail; and you, when once you have turned back, strengthen your brothers' (Luke 22:31-32).

Yes, the Pharisees and Scribes were right: 'This man welcomes sinners and eats with them' (Luke 15:2). To the end, and beyond.

'This is my Body for you, this is my Blood for you' (Luke 22:19-20)

A meal, the last meal, the last in a long history of shared meals. But also a meal which was unique: it crowned all the other meals, it achieved all that Jesus wanted to achieve from the very beginning of his ministry; it brought to fulfilment all that was 'promise' in Jesus' daily table-companionship.

'My Body..., my Blood, for you': Jesus, in Abba's name, wanted, in John's words, 'to gather together in unity God's scattered children' (John 11:52). In order to achieve his mission, he had taught his people, and 'revealed' God's name to them; he had healed the sick; he had comforted the afflicted; he had shared meals with people, he had been, constantly, 'for others', out of love. And now the moment was approaching when he would give his life for them, when in John's words, 'he would love them to the end' (John 13:1); and in the Upper Room, he already offered himself for the supreme sacrifice of his life: 'my Body..., my Blood for you'. He offered himself to be 'bread broken and shared' for the life of the world, so that the Kingdom of God might become reality; the Kingdom of justice, and peace, and forgiveness; Abba's Kingdom.

'Do this in memory of me'

'Do this in memory of me.' To whom were these words addressed? And what was their meaning? What is their meaning for us?

Matthew, Mark and Luke, in their story of the Last Supper, show us Jesus sitting at table with the 'apostles' (Luke), with the Twelve (Matthew and Mark). This does not mean that only the Twelve were sharing Jesus' last meal. But we can accept that the words 'Do this in memory of me' were directed first to the Twelve; Jesus entrusted his 'testament' to them, he wanted them to remember him, to remember his mission, his teaching; a 'memory' which would be expressed, in particular, in the disciples' communities, in the form of a meal, in the form of Jesus' last meal in the Upper Room. What better way to remember, to celebrate Jesus, the Jesus who 'welcomed sinners and ate with them', than a meal, a shared meal in the course of which the disciples would re-enact, in words and gestures, what Jesus had done and said in the Upper Room, and would therefore remember and celebrate all that Jesus had stood for, his person, his mission, and the crowning of his mission through his passion, death and resurrection?

'The Lord's Supper, also called 'the Breaking of Bread', or the 'Agapè' (the love-feast) seems to have found its place immediately in the very first Christian communities. In his first letter to the Christians of Corinth, written around the year 57 A.D., Paul challenges the Corinthians on the way they celebrate the Lord' s Supper (I Corinthians 11:17-32). And Luke sees in 'the Breaking of Bread', one of the major characteristics of the life of the Christian community in Jerusalem: 'Day by day, as they spent much time together in the temple, they broke bread at home and ate their food with glad and generous hearts, praising God and having the goodwill of all the people. And day by day the Lord added to their number those who were being saved' (Acts 2:46-47).

Thus, faithful to Jesus' command, 'do this in memory of me,' the apostles and their missionary helpers always communicated to the new communities they founded, Jesus' testament. The celebration of the Lord's Supper was truly one of the major hallmarks of the life of a Christian community.

A celebration which was not simply 'memory of the past' but entailed a renewed commitment to 'follow Jesus', to continue his mission, to be, as Jesus himself had been, 'disciples' who were 'bridge builders', unity-makers; disciples who, like Jesus 'welcomed sinners and ate with them.' And this is where we need to expose ourselves again and again to the challenge which the Eucharist offers us. We can so easily be content with taking part in the eucharist celebration, or in 'the eucharistic devotions' which have developed over the centuries without being sufficiently aware that the Jesus of the eucharist cannot but remind us that we must continue his mission. We must be, in the world, what Jesus himself was, servants and witnesses of the Kingdom of God, Abba's Kingdom; indefatigable servants and witnesses of Abba's immense kindness and compassion for the world. True, the eucharist is the food that is given to strengthen me, but it strengthens me so that I will continue my journey as a 'missionary' of God's love.

This is the criterion of the evangelical authenticity of our eucharistic celebrations: we cannot truly celebrate the Lord's Supper unless we are willing to 'discern the Body', as Paul puts it, the Body which is the community, our community; that is, to love it, to respect it, and to offer it the Good News of Jesus Christ.

We have been reflecting and praying at length on the Journey of Discipleship; guided by the gospels, we have followed Jesus from the Jordan River to Jerusalem, from Jesus' baptism to his last Passover. And as we 'followed' Jesus, we entered more deeply into the mystery of his person, of his message; we grew in the knowledge of the God Jesus revealed to us as Abba.

Through the celebration of the eucharist, Jesus the Risen Lord meets us again, and calls us, 'come, follow me, I will make you into fishers of people.' And as always, he shows us the way: 'do this in memory of me', be prepared, and willing to be today, 'bread broken and shared' for the life of the world.